# Susan McCracken

# For the Love of a Friend

Cover design by Jeffrey S. Dowers

Friends United Press
Richmond, Indiana 47374-1980

# *For the Love of a*
# *Friend*

## Susan McCracken 1994

F
~~Don~~
McC

A 98-49

# Copyright © 1994 Susan McCracken

All rights reserved. Written permission must be secured from the publisher to use or reproduce any part of this book, except for brief quotations in critical reviews or articles.

Printed in the United States of America.
Published by
Friends United Press
101 Quaker Hill drive
Richmond In 47374-1980

**Library of Congress Cataloging-in-Publication Data**

McCracken, Susan, 1950-
   For the Love of a Friend / Susan McCracken
       p.  cm.
   ISBN 0-944350-29-1
   1. Quakers—Iowa—History—19th century— Fiction.
2. Teenage girls—Iowa—Fiction. 3. Family —Iowa—
Fiction.
I. Title.
PS3563.C352485F6  1994
813.54—dc20                         94-7130
1st Reprint 1995

                                         **CIP**

This book is dedicated to my daughter,
Alisha,
whose countless hours of suggestions
and editing made it possible.

# Table of Contents

| | | |
|---|---|---|
| *Chapter One* | **Grandmother's Challenge** | 1 |
| *Chapter Two* | **Transition** | 7 |
| *Chapter Three* | **Birth of a Cabin** | 13 |
| *Chapter Four* | **Meeting** | 23 |
| *Chapter Five* | **Jezebel** | 31 |
| *Chapter Six* | **Good Friends** | 37 |
| *Chapter Seven* | **Education** | 45 |
| *Chapter Eight* | **Surprise Visitor** | 53 |
| *Chapter Nine* | **Treasure Hunter** | 63 |
| *Chapter Ten* | **Promise Fulfilled** | 73 |
| *Chapter Eleven* | **Choices** | 81 |
| *Chapter Twelve* | **A Letter From Heaven** | 89 |
| *Chapter Thirteen* | **Winter's Fury** | 95 |
| *Chapter Fourteen* | **Rescue the Perishing** | 105 |
| *Chapter Fifteen* | **New Beginnings** | 115 |
| *Chapter Sixteen* | **Gurney versus Wilbur** | 125 |
| *Chapter Seventeen* | **Signs of Strength** | 133 |
| *Chapter Eighteen* | **Love is Blind** | 143 |
| *Chapter Nineten* | **Till Death Do Us Part** | 153 |
| *Chapter Twenty* | **Peace and Promise** | 161 |

## Chapter 1

# Grandmother's Challenge
### Spring, 1843

Anger, excitement, and overwhelming sadness. How can a person feel all these emotions at the same time? I suppose some people feel that a young woman of the weak age of fourteen just naturally has strong feelings, which quite naturally she can't control! But I do not consider myself to be like everyone else! Hadn't Grandmother Burgess told me time and again that I was special, not like other simpering females my age? So why was I experiencing these feelings?

It is easy to explain the anger with just one word: Father. I'll never forget that blustery day last winter when he made the announcement. His tumultuous eyes were the only things that gave away the fact he was about to shatter our world as we knew it, for Father felt to express one's emotions was a sign of weakness, especially for the head of the house. But I knew by his eyes that we were in for something of major proportions!

"I've applied to the Richmond Meeting to be released from our committment here," Father began, "in order to help some of the new Societies in the state of Iowa. I am quite certain approval will be granted, and I believe we can begin to make plans to travel as soon as the spring weather permits. I shall expect each of you to look upon

1

*FOR THE LOVE OF A FRIEND*

this move as a mission to spread the gospel."

IOWA?! How could Father do this to us? Who would want to move to a place where there was nothing but trees, prairie grass, sloughs, and Indians? I loved our town of Richmond-in fact, to me it was the most modern city in Indiana! Streets lined with shops, perfect for browsing, though Friends bought only that which was necessary for our simple life style; our Meeting House; a library, which was a whole world in itself, one I often got lost in. How could Father ask us to leave? And there was Maude, my best friend in the whole world. Maude, whose laugh could cheer me even in the darkest hour. Maude, who shared all my hopes and dreams and fears! I could never say good-bye to her!

The more I thought about it, the more I was sure Mother would agree with me-after all, she had a nice, if plain home, and friends and neighbors she wouldn't want to abandon. Although Mother was often the quiet marriage partner, there was a solid strength in her tall, thin frame and she had been known to express her opinion when she felt strongly moved. Surely this would be a time for her to speak against Father's poor judgement.

Then there was my eight-year-old sister Abigail. Abigail and I were not always the closest of sisters. She was simply to young to share any deep thoughts. After all, child's concerns were certainly not those of a fourteen year old. But Abigail would surely be an ally in this battle of wills. School was a breeze for her and she had just won the district spelling bee. I was certain she would unite with Mother and me against Father's foolish notion...wouldn't she?

I knew the boys would side with Father. At the old age (or so he thought) of ten, Jacob was sure to think this moving idea was some great adventure. He loved exploring the area around Richmond with his friends, and a migration to Iowa would simply be another new land to

2

conquer.

The youngest member of the family, five-year-old Levi, would be the least help of all. Levi, whose big blue eyes and soft brown hair made him so adorable, was too young to reason with. Besides, he always copied anything his big brother set out to do.

"Mother," I had cautiously begun as soon as Father had departed after his earth-shattering pronouncement, "thee will speak to Father about this ridiculous fantasy of his and make him change his mind...won't thee? Someone must make him see how foolish it would be to simply leave everything we have here in Richmond to move to Iowa!"

It was several moments before Mother spoke, but as soon as she began, the resolute expression on her face smothered my hopes quicker than water on a fire. "Thee knows, Rebecca, that thy Father never decides anything of great importance without first spending great time in prayer followed by a confirmation of the Inner Light. For me to question his decision would be to question God himself, which of course I cannot do. There is also the matter of the confirmation of the Meeting, which I am sure will be granted." Then she added rather wistfully, her expression softening. "It would have been nice to have been able to remain here where we know everyone, but I am sure new challenges will be rewarding."

So much for Mother's support! Abigail probably wouldn't be much help either, I decided reluctantly, since she was an avid reader and adventure stories were her favorite. She'd probably only think of this as some great and glorious plot for her own writings some day. So I was left alone in my defense of keeping things the way they were; left alone to deal with the anger I felt toward Father for turning our lives upside down.

In the end it was Grandma Wilson, Father's mother, who helped me conquer the surging feelings of anger.

*FOR THE LOVE OF A FRIEND*

There was no one who had experienced more anger and hurt than Grandma, and yet she had been able to overcome all of it. Her husband had been jailed for helping move slaves to freedom on the Underground Railroad, then eventually had died in an accident, again trying to free black people. She had lost three babies to illnesses when she first came to Indiana, and, in fact Father was her only child to grow to adulthood. And she was even now beginning to lose her eyesight and would eventually be unable to see at all. Anger, however, was never seen in Grandma. When I had asked her one day why she seldom became angry, she was quick to reply, "I learned a long time ago, Rebecca, that anger is the devil's work, and I refuse to be a part of it. The Word says, "My God shall supply all your need according to his riches in glory in Christ Jesus," and I have always trusted in God. Good things have always come from my sorrow, the greatest being my four wonderful grandchildren." Then Grandma continued, "Thee must forget the past, Rebecca, and the things thee cannot change, and look forward to what God has in store for thee!"

That was easy for Grandma to say-she was an old woman!! I knew I shouldn't be angry, but I suppose I still was. Of course, as the long days of winter began to pass and more preparations for our journey were made, excitement began to slowly replace some of the anger. What would it be like to pack everything in a wagon and move? Would there be other girls my age? Would there be boys? (Of course I would not ask that question of anyone, as it was not proper for a young lady to be thinking such thoughts!) Would I have my own room? And what would I put in it if I couldn't take all my possessions? Would there be any social gatherings? Quilting or husking bees? I became less angry, and thoughts of moving began to occupy my mind more often.

4

*Grandmother's Challenge*

Once the approval from the Friends Meeting was granted for our move, the feelings of sadness began. How could I leave my grandparents? My best friend Maude? Richmond was the only place I had ever lived, the only school I had ever attended was there. And our Friends at Meeting. How could we leave them when they were so much like family?

Father's surprise announcement in March that Grandma Wilson would be moving with us due to the condition of her eyesight helped ease my heavy heart just a bit, as did the promises of my friends to write, and even visit some day if possible. I suppose sadness is something one must let slowly fade away, much like the bright blue of denim as the wash gradually erases the color. I hoped it wouldn't take too long!


The final days before our journey were as you might expect: full. Full of disagreements about what could be taken and what would have to be left behind. Full of visits with friends we might very well never see again, full of promises to write, promises to remember, promises to pray. The days were so full, in fact, I hardly had time to feel any of my previous emotions. I had finally accepted the fact we were migrating, and was almost to the point of looking forward to the challenges of the new life before us. It probably meant the most to me when the Meeting held a commissioning service for our family, as well as for the two other families also setting out for Iowa. Being a member of the Society of Friends, or Quakers as we were sometimes called, meant being a part of a group of believers who felt that each person was important in the body of Christ. When several families left, it was like losing a part of the body. I cannot really explain how I felt that day as Friends surrounded us and gave us their blessings, but it was a wonderful feeling of belonging, and

*FOR THE LOVE OF A FRIEND*

a great sadness of having to separate from the group. We were reminded of the new meetings we would be supporting, and the prayers we would each say for the other. It was the final act of severing our ties with the past and looking to the future.

Maude and I made great promises to each other: to write, pray, and visit the first chance we had. We had spent many hours together the past several years sharing our hopes and dreams, and we had also discussed every boy in the Richmond Meeting-none of which we thought worthy of us! Would I ever find another friend like Maude? I seriously doubted it!

Hardest of all was saying farewell to Grandmother Burgess. Tears streamed from my eyes like water from a sprinkling can as I held her so tightly she nearly gasped for air! "We shall meet again, my dear, "Grandmother whispered, "if not in this life, then in Heaven. It is a great challenge to help begin a new Meeting, and thou art blessed of God and destined to do great things! Don't ever let anyone think less of thee because thee is a woman. Remember, 'God created them equal, male and female created He them!' I shall await our reunion some day with great anticipation to learn what thee has accomplished for our Lord!"

A warmth spread throughout my soul as Grandmother's words soothed my fears and doubts. I would simply have to see what God had in store for me, Rebecca Wilson: Friend, woman, child of God!

**Chapter 2**

# Transition

We had been traveling for what seemed like an eternity, although Father would not care for me using that expression! My feet felt as if they could not possibly travel another inch on the hard ground with the sun beating down on me! Abigail, Jacob, Levi and I had to walk beside the covered wagon while Mother and Father rode in front. Grandma Wilson had announced at the last minute that she had no intention of starting life over at her age, and she flatly refused to be persuaded to make the journey with us to Iowa. I really admired Grandma for standing up to Father and doing what she felt best. Another lesson to store in my memory for future reference!

I preferred to be outside walking, though there was really no choice in the matter. We had so many belongings in the wagon there was simply no room to sit, as well as the fact that it was unbearably warm under the cover. By walking along side the slow-moving wagon, I could explore the area as we passed. I was continually amazed at the beauty of the land: the majestic trees, leaves wavering in the breeze, and the bubbling streams tripping over stones singing out God's praise. In the days preceeding our departure, I had imagined what our trail would look like; never, however, had I imagined what was reality! My mind had pictured long stretches of grassy prairie with not a tree in sight. Indiana and Illinois provided some flat

7

*FOR THE LOVE OF A FRIEND*

areas where the tall grasses waved in the breeze, but more numerous were the hills and valleys, wooded areas and streams. And I never tired of admiring the beauty around me-except those times, such as now, when my feet shouted their misery so loud all else seemed unimportant!

The other two families making the journey with us were the Fraziers and the Hocketts. Like our family, they each had felt the moving of the Holy Spirit during Meeting and volunteered to move to Iowa. The Fraziers had two children: Sarah, who was just a sweet, though sometimes screaming baby, and Joshua, who was fifteen, and someone I rather disliked. The Hocketts were the parents of three girls, ages seven, eight, and ten. Although our age differences prevented close friendships, I enjoyed walking with these others as we would make up stories about our new homes and pretend we were hiding from the wild Indians. I must admit we knew very little about Indians-only what we had read in books and the descriptions our teachers had given us. I had an idea they weren't quite as savage as we were pretending them to be! As Friends, we believed in the oneness of all men, regardles of skin color. Hadn't we done everything possible to help free the Negroes from the bonds of slavery? Were the Redmen any less in God's eyes? I would have to ponder that thought before confronting the other children!

My feet were not getting any better. I had tried taking my shoes off to ease the pain, only to be scolded by Father for being so naive. (How was I to know my tender feet would never last in the tough prairie grass?!) I was now left to limping, hoping we would set up camp soon so my weary feet could at last find rest.

"Hey Becky—whatsa matter? Can't thee walk even one day's journey?"

I knew immediately who was behind those taunting remarks-Joshua Frazier! He knew from talking with my brother Jacob that I loathed being called 'Becky', which I suspected was the reason he persisted in addressing me in that manner.

*Transition*

I had always felt that when one was named after a great woman in the Bible, it was disrespectful to shorten the name!

It was generally understood among the adults that Joshua and I did not enjoy each other's company. Having heard us argue several times over the course of our travels, they usually tried to assign the tasks so we had little or no contact with each other. As far as I was concerned, Joshua was a big-mouthed know-it-all, one who did not exhibit the characteristics of Friends: simplicity, kindness, and caring for the well-being of others. No, Joshua represented none of those Christian attitudes, and I couldn't wait until we reached Iowa and went our separate ways!

"Oh Becky, is thee hard of hearing? What is thee limping for?" he persisted.

"Joshua, I would appreciate it if thee would address me by my given name, Rebecca," I finally answered icily.

"Why is thee so touchy about thy name?" Joshua continued. "So I shorten it by one little syllable! Thee still knows I am talking to thee, so what is the reason for thy anger?"

Trying to explain something to Joshua was next to impossible, since he never seemed to really listen to me. I found that ignoring him was the best approach, since it made him very angry! Let him talk to himself if he couldn't use my three syllable name!

"Becky Wilson, thee is the most impossible girl I know! Thee just confirms my opinion of women-all are hopeless! I hope thy feet swell up as big as thy head!"

Poor Joshua. He would probably never understand women! I pitied the poor woman who chose to be his wife!


The days passed into weeks as we continued our slow journey westward. Father made sure every night when we set up camp that each family knew exactly where we were on the journey, and was always generous with his praise for the cooperation of each member of the group. I understood and felt the respect the others had for Father, and couldn't help but feel pride in the leadership role he had assumed. Father was not always easy for me to understand, though; at times he was a figure of authority, commanding other's respect and admiration. Yet at other times he seemed so strict and unyielding, much like the blacksmith's anvil where white hot iron was molded into form by the pounding hammer. Perhaps Father was trying to mold and shape his family by being the anvil for our lives. I often wished he showed the same respect for my concerns and needs as he did for the rules and regulations he felt we all should respect. I kept these feelings to myself, however, as I knew disrespect would be the label Father would attach to these thoughts.

Joshua and I continued to avoid each other, and thus the days were pleasant, full of new things to see and learn. Anticipation of our journey's end grew stronger each day, and each member of the group was feeling quite jovial. We would often sing favorite hymns to pass the time, especially in the evenings around the campfire. Hymns of joy and thanksgiving for our safety thus far were our best-loved. I could sing the melody, but preferred to sing harmony, enjoying the way the sounds blended together. I suppose some might consider it vanity, but I thought I had a pretty singing voice, especially when combined with the others. Once, when we were singing a particularly moving song of God's faithfulness, I happened to glance at Joshua. Rather than the usual teasing glint in his deep brown eyes, there appeared to be a glimmer of adoration as he gazed at me. Seeing me turn his way, however, he quickly stuck out his tongue and made a face, doubling over with laughter when I walked away disgustedly. If I were his parents, I'd be embarrassed to have raised such a deplorable character!

The stars were shining brightly on the last night of our journey. I could not sleep for the excitement that filled my

*Transition*

soul. We had crossed the mighty roaring Mississippi, taking a ferry at a town called Muscatine. It was more than a little scary as the swirling muddy water lapped the ferry, rocking it dangerously. We each breathed a sigh of relief when our feet touched the Iowa soil. Tomorrow we would travel southwest to our new meeting at East Grove, but tonight we were camped outside the town of Salem, the first Friend's settlement west of the Mississippi.

It's hard to describe the sense of accomplishment and pride we all felt as we walked the dusty streets of Salem that first day in our new territory. Although we knew our work was not yet begun, we couldn't help but feel good about reaching our destination-or close to it, anyway. That feeling of accomplishment was probably what helped ease the disappointment in the discovery of what a new settlement town was like. Salem was nothing at all like Richmond! In fact, had Salem been but one day's journey from Richmond instead of many weeks, I would probably have looked scornfully upon the worn dirt path between the few crude buildings that constituted the simple stores of Salem. Our travels, however, had helped cushion the shocking comparison of Richmond and Salem.

Father and the other men had located the general store soon after our arrival and secured the supplies they would need for their new beginnings, a plow being the most important purchase for breaking the tangled roots of tough prairie sod. The women and children sought and quickly found the Salem meeting house where several members were gathered for a time of prayer for the safety of Friends traveling from the East. Imagine their surprise when they found us waiting for them outside the doors when they finished! These Friends were so glad to see us that we felt like celebrities instead of the disheveled, dusty travelers we all were. They were suprised we had arrived so quickly, but soon it seemed like we had known each other for years instead of minutes. That was another thing I had noticed about Friends: the warmth they

11

*FOR THE LOVE OF A FRIEND*

radiated and their ability to make everyone feel at ease. It was good to spend time with Friends, to learn about the successes-and sometimes failures-of the new meetings we were to support. We felt united in our beliefs and mission.

As I lay shivering in the cool May air that night, I couldn't help but experience some of those same feelings that had filled my thoughts that day we had departed westward on our journey. As I pondered what lay ahead for each of us, I was more than a little apprehensive! And I was still excited, even more so now that we were almost there! But surprisingly, it was now difficult to remember why I had been so angry. There had been periods of sadness throughout the seven week journey, especially when I remembered something Grandmother Burgess had said, or when I thought of trying to survive without my best friend, Maude. But I no longer felt overwhelmed when I considered the future. What did God have in store for my life? Would I recognize the Inner Light of God within me and follow His leading?

Questions continued to swirl in my mind like the fast moving Mississippi we had crossed earilier in the day. Long after the others were asleep, I was still pondering the events of the past seven weeks. Tomorrow would be the beginning of the answers, and I couldn't wait to see what was in store for the Wilson family!

**Chapter 3**

# Birth of a Cabin

H ey Becky...would thee PLEASE come help me roll this log?" teased Joshua. "It's so heavy and I need thy help!" Joshua needed my help like he needed a hole in the head (and sometimes I thought he had one!) The "log" was a mere sapling to be used for the roof of our new cabin, and even five-year-old Levi could have carried it! Joshua, on the other hand, was big for his fifteen years, nearly as tall as Father. His dark unruly curls were seldom combed, and he reminded me somewhat of a child just awakening from a nightmare! I suppose some girls might have found him attractive-that is until they got to know him!

"I would think such a strong BOY as thee would certainly be able to carry a mere twig such as that!" I replied in my sweetest voice. Joshua thought of himself as a man, and to be called a boy was just about more than he could bear!

"Why doesn't thee go help the women prepare the noon meal for those of us who are WORKING!" was Joshua's not too pleasant retort. Smiling to myself over my small victory, I turned to my task at hand: bringing a bucket of water to Mother and the other women who were slaving over the hot fire preparing a meal of fresh venison stew for the workers. Once again the female mind had prevailed over the know-it-all of the likes of Joshua Frazier!

Cabin raising, I had discovered, was one of the more

13

*FOR THE LOVE OF A FRIEND*

exciting things to occur in a new land. When we had arrived at East Grove in May, there was nothing but prairie grass and trees everywhere one looked. Despair had filled my soul as I remembered our nice home in Richmond, simple but furnished in good taste, and the possessions I had been forced to leave behind. Now we were faced with no place to even lay our heads at night! Father, Mother, Abigail, Jacob, Levi and I had all worked until we were ready to collapse each night to make a lean-to in the side of a hill by a crystal clear stream running through the middle of our new land. It looked extremely primitive to me, but I suppose Father was right in feeling it would meet our needs until a cabin could be built. I'll never forget that first terrifying night in the lean-to, partially because my body refused to go to sleep, and partially because of the rodents I just knew were going to crawl all over my tender young body. We had seen several rats and mice as we burrowed into their homes to build our shelter, not to mention hundreds of beetles, worms, and the like, which came crawling and squirming from the rich black soil. I must admit the mind can play some pretty mean tricks on a person, but it still took me nearly a week to become comfortable enough to sleep through the night! Abigail and I shared a "bed", consisting of several layers of leaves and prairie grass, as did the boys and Father and Mother. I'm sure on several occasions when I abruptly sat up in bed thinking the worst, it was only Abigail bumping into me, or I her.

I would hate to admit it to a living soul, but I actually grew quite fond of the lean-to, as it became a cozy spot to visit with Mother as we prepared the meals on the campfire just in front of the homey structure. I admired Mother's ability to adjust to her new surroundings with a calm assurance I did not possess. I also knew she was often pondering much deeper subjects than what to fix for the next meal! We would discuss the new neighbors we had just met, or how we would furnish our soon-to-be-built cabin, or even the latest theological thoughts of George Fox or Joseph John Gurney. We were

*Birth of a Cabin*

careful to keep our discussions quiet, however, as Father did not necessarily approve of women discussing religion!

Now, as July was rapidly approaching, we were to finally have our new cabin, a place to really call our own. In comparision to the lean-to, it seemed almost a mansion, though in reality it would be little more than a small crude structure!

We had done much in preparation for the cabin raising. Father and the boys had spent long hours in the dense woods beyond our lean-to with their axes, felling both large and small trees. After trimming and notching them, the heavy logs were dragged to the place we had chosen for the cabin with the team of oxen. Choosing the cabin sight had been easy: there was a slight rise in the ground a few hundred yards from the creek, making it safe from flooding with a wonderful view of the surrounding area. There were many wooded areas where the stands of oak, maple and elm trees blotted out the horizon, but there were also clear areas where the prairie grasses and wild flowers decorated the landscape like a beautiful painting. Just the sight of it filled my heart with praise which often led to a song I couldn't contain! We had rolling hills and a creek, and in my opinion, God had created everything perfectly on our homestead!

The first day we had arrived at East Grove, Father had carefully driven our wagon to this area. Stepping off 1500 paces each direction, he proceeded to drive four corner stakes to mark our claim, covering approximately 320 acres. Five acres had been painstakingly broken with the plow Father purchased in Salem, thus protecting our land by showing proof of ownership. The other two families had done likewise in their new settlements: the Fraziers at New Garden and the Hocketts at Chestnut Hill. Cabins had already been built for the others, and it was finally our turn.

I was surprised by the number of families who had driven here to help us build on this sweltering day. We had had very little contact with others living in our area, with the exception

*FOR THE LOVE OF A FRIEND*

being Meeting on Sundays. Thus to see twenty families arrive ready and eager to do their share was a real blessing!

By noon the walls were nearly completed, using ramps to roll the highest logs to the tops of each side. I could see Joshua still dragging the saplings for the roof, but for once he seemed too involved with his work to needle me with his endless taunts. I noticed there was another young man working with Joshua that I had not seen before, but I decided he was someone I would have to be introduced to one way or the other! Having just passed my fifteenth birthday, I felt it was time to be on the lookout for eligible marriage prospects. Of course, I would have received a long lecture from Father or Mother had they any idea such thoughts were on my mind! I think they expected me to be an old maid of twenty before thinking of marriage. Perhaps I was rushing things a bit, but that young man certainly looked interesting.

When Mother asked me to return to the creek for yet another bucket of water, I couldn't help but time my trip when I thought Joshua and his friend would be crossing my path with yet another load of saplings.

"Joshua," I called as I neared the area where the two young men were working, my bucket brimming with thirst quenching water, "thee looks hot, as does thy friend. Would thee both care for a cool drink from the creek?"

A smug look appeared on his face as he set the young trees down for a moment. "Well, well...if it isn't little Miss Sunshine!" Joshua said with that irksome grin of his. "I was hoping thee would return and help me with my load, but a drink of cool water would do just as well!"

Leave it to Joshua to misinterpret my mission! "Would thee please introduce thy workmate, Joshua? Where are thy manners?!" I chided, feeling quite exasperated!

"Why Becky! I didn't think thee was interested in boys like us!"

"Joshua," I retorted, unable to restrain my anger a second longer, "sometimes I wish I had never met thee! I have tried

16

*Birth of a Cabin*

to be civil to thee, and have made a simple request, but if thee cannot be polite enough to introduce thy friend, I shall have to take this bucket of water to Mother immediately!"

"All right," Joshua replied reluctantly, thirst getting the better of him. "This is John Shipling. John, this is Becky Wilson. It is for her family that we are building the cabin."

John walked toward me, a warm smile accompanying the twinkle in his deep blue eyes. He was much taller than Joshua, though his boyish features made it difficult to guess his age. "Pleased to make your acquaintance, Rebecca," John said as he extended his hand. I had never shaken any man's hand before, so I was not sure if it was proper for me to do so. But hadn't Father taught us never to be rude to any other person? Surely it would not be polite to let John stand there forever with his hand extended!

Tentatively, I reached forward and took his hand in mine. His handshake was firm and a bit sweaty, but I cannot deny that I enjoyed it just a bit!

"John and his father live a quarter of a mile from our cabin," Joshua continued, "and are members of the Mormons.

His mother died with the ague a year ago, so it is just the two of them. They may be heading West within the next year to join other Mormons in their journey to Salt Lake City."

"Does thee want to leave this area?" I asked, looking curiously at John. I was a bit disappointed to discover he was not a Friend, but that didn't seem to prevent the warm feelings I felt toward this tall stranger. "Yes and no," John replied after thinking for a while. "I really enjoy the peacefulness of the quiet streams and woods of Iowa. I take pleasure in fishing in the summer and hunting deer and turkey in the winter, but I sense that my father is not happy here. I know he misses my mother a great deal..." John paused as he shuffled his feet among the broken twigs from the many limbs that had been carried that morning. "If it would make Father happy to move, then I would want to go with him. Being sixteen, I could stay here in the cabin and probably work the soil for a living, but

17

*FOR THE LOVE OF A FRIEND*

it would mean sending Father on alone, and I simply could not do that!"

"See Becky, some of us men have a sense of responsibility!" Joshua interjected, rather haughtily.

"Yes, Joshua, I find John's feelings for his father to be quite honorable," I replied, looking again at John's handsome though temporarily saddened face.

A smile began to brighten John's features as he looked up and began to really notice me for the first time.

"Thank you, Rebecca, for those kind words. Do you mind if I use your full name?"

"Actually, I would prefer being called Rebecca, John," I said as I looked triumphantly at Joshua, who seemed to have developed a sour look all of a sudden!

"Well, Joshua," John finally said after an uneasy pause, "I think we had best get our drink Rebecca has so kindly brought us, and get back to work."

"I suppose thee is right. Thanks for the water, Becky. Thee can bring me a drink any time!"

Now I was certain there was not a brain in Joshua's head! Couldn't he figure it out that it was John that interested me? Looking purposely in John's deep blue eyes and smiling what I hoped to be my most winning smile, I picked up the bucket and started for the creek to refill it once again with the cool water.

Yes, living in Iowa was certainly taking a turn for the better! John Shipling was someone I hoped to run into again, preferably without that awful Joshua Frazier present. I would have to keep his acquaintance a secret for now...I was quite certain Father would not approve of my being interested in a Mormon! But it could certainly do no harm to get to know a person before one dismissed him as unsuitable!


The next few weeks following the cabin raising seemed to fly by as there was a great deal of work to be completed once

*Birth of a Cabin*

the frame was in place. We children were in charge of securing clay mud from the sloping creek banks to use for chinking between the logs. At first it was great fun as more and more mud squished between our toes and found itself being tossed from one sibling to another! As the days wore on, however, I began to dread yet another walk to the now extremely slick creek bank for yet another heavy load of clay. Prairie grass had to be kneaded into the mud before wedging it between the logs, and my arms and legs ached each night as I would lie thinking about my new life.

The best part of the new cabin, in my opinion, was the loft where we children slept. We had one opening on the south wall just under the peak of the roof that I considered my window to the world. Father had carefully packed three glass windows from Richmond to be used in our new home, one of which was the small one in our room. I will always be grateful to Father for respecting his children enough to provide this source of light instead of the oil cloth that would normally cover such an opening. As we were expected to retire to the loft early each night, I found it a great pleasure to gaze through this window to the world beyond and imagine what life held for me. Abigail would sometimes sit with me and we would share our innermost thoughts with each other. At the age of eight, however, her concerns were seldom mine!

Abigail was so pretty, and so smart that I might have been jealous if she had been closer to my age. Her features were as beautiful as some of the porcelain dolls I had seen in the Richmond store windows. Because of her young age, I could admire her good qualities and let it go at that.

The floor of our one room cabin was still dirt, but Father promised a plank floor as soon as the harvest of the wheat was completed. Jacob was in charge of sweeping the floor each day once the chinking was completed. It was quite a job as we women were not pleased with dust in our prepared food!

The furnishings were simple: a corner bed for Father and Mother, a wooden table and a chair for each of us, and

*FOR THE LOVE OF A FRIEND*

Mother's spinning wheel. The fireplace covered nearly half the north wall where shelves would eventually be built for our small supply of kitchen utensils. I did not enjoy the fireplace at first, as working every morning over the fire was an extremely hot and tiring job. Mother assured me we would appreciate it's warmth in January, and I reluctantly agreed, though right now it seemed the fires of hell could not have been hotter!

Sweat was running down my neck and back one Saturday as I prepared provisions for the upcoming Sabbath. Levi came bursting into the cabin and threw his chubby arms around my legs.

"Rebecca! Rebecca!" he squealed excitedly, "Guess what?"

Levi's chubby cheeks were flushed from his running, and his dark eyes spoke of a hidden secret I must discover. Levi and I enjoyed each other's company on most occasions, but there were times I wished he would simply say what was on his childish mind instead of expecting me to guess! Being in no mood to play games, I replied rather sharply, "What does thee want, Levi? Can't thee see I'm trying to get ready for Sabbath?"

Suddenly looking defeated, Levi's arms slowly dropped to his side and his quivering chin sank to his chest. I felt badly for hurting his feelings with my sharp tongue and lashing words. Dropping to my knees, I put my arms around him to find out what he had been so anxious for me to discover.

"What is it, Levi?" I tried to sound at least a little excited.

Perking up, he tried again. "Rebecca, does thee know tomorrow is Monthly Meeting and we get to have a picnic dinner?!"

Personally, Monthly Meeting was not something I usually got excited about. Conducting the business of East Grove Friends Meeting was often a long hot ordeal. As a fifteen-year-old, I was expected to attend the session in the stifling meeting house. Levi, on the other hand, would get to stay

20

*Birth of a Cabin*

outside and play quietly with the younger children.

"I had almost forgotten, Levi. I'm glad thee reminded me. Thee had best tell Jacob to begin carrying water for our baths. Thee wouldn't want to go to Meeting dirty!"

At this bit of news, Levi quickly took off running. I had a feeling he might somehow "forget" to tell Jacob about the bath water! It did start me thinking about tomorrow's meeting. Having a noon carry-in dinner with the other members would be interesting. I was anxious to get to know some of the other girls my age, and this would give us more time to get acquainted. I was sure Mother had simply forgotten to mention Monthly Meeting to me, but just in case it had slipped her mind, I decided to find her and see what she had planned for us to take. It would be nice having something to look forward to once again! Maybe another new family would have arrived from the East...maybe a family with a son my age?!

# Chapter 4

# Meeting

R ebecca, I will expect thee outside the cabin in five minutes to leave for meeting!" came Father's loud booming voice. Father was not a very large man, but he certainly had a large, and at this point rather impatient voice!

Deciding what to wear to meeting was not difficult. Gray dress, gray stockings, topped off with a gray scuttle-shaped bonnet. When George Fox, the founder of the Society of Friends, had organized his followers, one of the testimonies he insisted on was simplicity. He felt that Elizabeth and James I, as well as many of their fellow Englishmen, were more interested in looking extravagant than in worshiping God. For Fox, the simple gray clothing was the Quaker's badge to distinguish them from other religious persons. Simplicity was also to protect them from the evil influences of the world.

When members of the Society of Friends had arrived in America, they kept many of George Fox's beliefs; thus my choice of what to wear was not a choice at all! I secretly felt that if Fox had been a female, perhaps he would have been just a bit more lenient toward women's dresses! Men had little variety anyway, gray trousers and gray shirts being the dress for any occasion. We women, on the other hand, needed a bit of color when the entire dress was one solid piece! I just didn't quite understand how a little color was going to harm my relationship with God.

*FOR THE LOVE OF A FRIEND*

I had mentioned this idea to Mother once when we had been shopping in Richmond. I had seen a bolt of a very lovely shade of violet that I thought would contrast quite nicely with the gray. Mother's reaction to my suggestion that we buy a few yards, however, led me to believe there must be more to this idea of simplicity than I understood!

No, choice of clothing was not my problem this morning. I'm not sure why it was taking me so long to dress. I suppose I just wanted to look my best in case there were new families at meeting that I had not met. I spent a long time combing my thick, waist-length hair, although it would be tucked in my bonnet where neatness was unimportant. Perhaps I was day-dreaming a bit...the handsome face of John Shipling crossed my mind and I wondered if he were going to his church this Sabbath. I knew very little about the Mormon religion, except that Friends didn't think too highly of it. I wondered if I would ever see him again, and if I did, would he be the least bit interested in me.

I was not what you would call beautiful, but I certainly wasn't homely, either. I thought my hazel eyes and brown hair were rather plain, but maybe that made me a good Quaker! I was putting my shoes on when Father's booming voice came up the ladder to the loft once more.

"Rebecca, does thee want to ride to meeting or does thee prefer to walk? We are departing immediately!"

Hurrying down the from the loft, I ran to the wagon just as Father was urging the new team of Belgian horses on. Father felt being punctual was important in God's eyes, and he was seldom late for anything. I was glad I had gotten to the wagon on time, as it was three miles to the meeting house and I had no desire to walk that far this morning.

The "road" we took was very rough from the many times heavy wagons had traveled the worn path during the wet months of spring, often cutting ruts up to the wheel axles. The hot sun of July had baked the deep channels until they were brick hard, thus our extremely bumpy ride! It was even

*Meeting*

difficult to talk to the other children, although we tried to carry on a conversation to make the trip go a little faster. This morning we were comparing life in Iowa to life in Richmond. I was surprised to hear first Abigail, then Jacob, and finally Levi tell how much they enjoyed life in our cabin and surrounding woods and prairie. I had to agree that I enjoyed the quiet peacefulness of our new home, but I also missed the bustle of the city with its rows of shops and people. We all agreed we would like to see other young people more often, and we thought Father and Mother could let up just a little on the work. Basically, however, we were happy with our new lives.

As we approached the long log building that was the East Grove Meeting House, we could see a number of wagons already present. Father left our wagon under a tree with ample foliage to shade the picnic dinner we had brought, then unhitched the horses and staked them to graze. We would be here nearly all day, catching up on business, both meetingwise and peoplewise. As I was climbing down from the tall wagon, I noticed a familiar-looking family approaching. From a distance, it almost looked like the Fraziers. I knew that was not possible, however, since they had settled in the New Garden area to help support that meeting. I decided it must be some family I had yet to meet, but one I would make sure to become acquainted with at the picnic.

The meeting house was certainly plain, in keeping with Friends beliefs. It was a low, rectangular building with plain glass windows. In the front were two solid doors, the one on the right for men, on the left for women. I suppose the simplicity of the building was to reflect the Friends' belief that God lives within the person, not in the building. To a stranger, it would simply look like a long cabin.

As I was about to reach the entrance for women, a now all too familiar voice greeted me, one I had hoped to forget.

"Becky! Thee looks especially nice this morning!" came the teasing words from Joshua.

25

"Joshua Frazier, what is thee doing here?! I thought thy family was helping support the New Garden Meeting," I said, surprise and annoyance coloring my voice.

"Well, we were, for a while. We had been meeting in member's homes for worship since there were not enough to support building a Meeting House. The elders finally decided there were too many Mormons in our area to have a vital meeting, so they agreed each family would try to support one of the other Friends groups close to us." Joshua paused as if thinking how to finish. "Since we live about the same distance from East Grove as New Garden, this is our best choice. Thee doesn't mind, does thee?"

"Thee can worship wherever thee likes, Joshua. I really don't care," I said crisply, then added rather reluctantly, "I suppose the other members will be glad to have thy families' support."

I immediately entered the left door, effectively ending my conversation with Joshua. Why did he seem to always show up when I least expected, or wanted, to see him?!

Inside the meeting house it was quiet and calm. Rows of simple, flat benches made up the furnishings. There were no pictures, lamps, or ornaments in keeping with simplicity. The front bench was on a raised platform for the elders.

It always took me a while to "center down", as Friends called it. I was never quite certain what centering down meant, but I believed it included trying to clear one's mind of daily matters (like finding out Joshua would be attending our meeting), and trying to listen for the voice of the Holy Spirit. We could sometimes hear one of the men's loud voices through the partition which separated the men and women, but generally it was quiet. Sometimes a woman would stand and speak a message from the Holy Spirit, and at other times someone might offer a quiet prayer. When that happened, we were all expected to rise and stand quietly. I was rather grateful when someone felt led to pray, as the wooden planks got very hard and it was a relief to stand. We were expected

*Meeting*

to sit quietly in the silence. Every once in a while I would see Abigail get a bit fidgety, and Mother's hand would gently rest on her leg until she was quiet.

I hoped someday I would feel a message from the Holy Spirit and be moved to speak aloud. At the age of fifteen, I was not yet considered ready to speak, but there were times when I was sure I felt the Holy Spirit within me during worship.

After some three hours had passed, the women in the front rose and we knew worship was finished. I often wondered why it was necessary to spend three long hours in worship, but it was one of those things I knew better than to question!

Helping Mother, we got our dinner of wild turkey and stuffing laid out with the others on the side boards of several wagons. It looked like a feast to most of us, and I couldn't wait to try some of the delicious-looking dishes I had never seen before. After the meal, the women would share recipes, and I wanted to make sure Mother got some new ones to add a little variety to our meals. Our food at home was good, but limited. We had very little garden produce due to our busy time after arriving in May.

I had just finished filling my plate when I saw Joshua approaching. He saw me before I could duck behind the wagon.

"Becky, would thee like to share my blanket?" he asked.

"I would rather eat with a rattlesnake than eat with thee!" I snapped, annoyed at being caught.

"Rebecca, thee will not speak to our friends in that manner!" came Father's grim judgment from behind.

I knew I would receive some type of discipline when I returned home if I didn't do something to rectify the situation immediately. Using my most apologetic tone, I said quietly, "What I meant to say, was that I would be afraid of sitting on a blanket for fear of rattlesnakes."

Father nodded and walked away, but not before giving me a stern look as if to warn me to behave in a proper manner.

With a smug look on his face, knowing he had won this

27

*FOR THE LOVE OF A FRIEND*

round, Joshua replied, "We can always sit in a wagon, Becky, if thee is afraid of snakes. Would thee like to sit in thy wagon or ours?"

Knowing I was cornered, I began to climb into our wagon before Joshua could extend his hand to help me, I was burning with anger but trying not to let it show.

Lunch went as well as could be expected under the circumstances, although I hardly tasted my food. I let Joshua talk on and on, as he was prone to do, and that way I didn't have to pretend to enjoy my dinner. As soon as I was finished, I quickly excused myself and hastily climbed out of the wagon to join the women in the recipe exchange. When I happened to look back at our wagon, Joshua was still sitting there with that same smug look on his face.

You may have won this time, Joshua Frazier, but I'll be more careful next time. I hope you enjoyed our first and only dinner together.

As I approached the gathering of women, I noticed a slender, extremely pretty young woman I had never seen before. She must have arrived earlier than our family, and with my unfortunate dinner experience with Joshua, I had not noticed her. I quickly positioned myself to speak to her, as I was not known for my shyness.

"How art thou? I did not notice thee this morning. Does thee live nearby? With thy family, I mean!" Leave it to me to speak before thinking."Yes, I and we do!" she said with a quick grin. I could see right away we were going to get along quite well.

"My name is Elizabeth, but I detest such a long name. My mother began calling me Betty when I was a baby, and I have been called that ever since. What else would thee like to know about me?" she asked with a twinkle in her eye.

"Well...I...," it was probably the first time in my life I had been at a loss for words. There were hundreds of things I wanted to know about this Betty, but now I was too embarrassed to ask. Fortunately, we were called to return to the

28

Meetinghouse for monthly meeting before I had to think of a quick reply.

I recovered my tongue as we were walking the short distance to the meeting house together. "Oh...my name is Rebecca, and I like long names, and I hope we may become friends...if thee would like to."

"I know thy name, Rebecca. I asked Joshua earlier to introduce us, but he muttered something about snakes and took off! We just arrived from Indiana a few weeks ago, so we have been too busy trying to get settled to meet many new friends. I will look forward to spending some time with thee soon, as we live only two miles east of thy homestead," Betty finished as we entered the building. Meeting Betty had greatly improved my disposition, and now I had something to look forward to besides more teasing from Joshua.

Monthly meeting took place in the afternoon with the same arrangement as during worship: men on one side, women on the other. The only difference being the use of sliding wooden shutters for business concerning both the men and women. The main order of business today was the report of the nominating committee, the group of members who appointed friends to the various positions of leadership in the meeting. As Father had been an elder in our Richmond Friends Meeting, he was nominated to fill a similar position here at East Grove. Father was a good elder, in my opinion, because he always tried to treat everyone fairly, and make decisions which would benefit the meeting as a whole.

I had trouble keeping my mind centered on the business at hand due to my unfortunate experience with Joshua at noon. I would have trouble forgiving him for putting me in the position he did. Why couldn't he be a gentleman like John Shipling? John would never have forced me into sharing a meal with him, not that he would have needed to!

The meeting seemed to drone on and on. There was discussion of Joseph John Gurney and his positive influence on Friends, and a sound denouncement of the teachings of

*FOR THE LOVE OF A FRIEND*

Elias Hicks. Hicks had been a powerful Friends minister in Long Island, New York, who eventually traveled far and wide spreading his views. Hicks taught Friends that the Light within was the only thing necessary for salvation and that Jesus was only superior because he had superior work to do. Father called him a humanist who taught rationalistic thought. I wasn't sure what that meant, but it didn't sound like the doctrine practiced by Friends that I had experienced.

Father told us later that he had spoken to the meeting regarding Elias Hicks and his followers, or Hicksites, as they were known. There had been some discussion following his words, and a minute had been recorded by the recording clerk stating East Grove's disapproval of Hick's teachings.

When Monthly Meeting was completed, many families stood visiting with each other. They were always reluctant to separate and go back to their solitary lives on their home-steads. It was nearly dusk when we climbed on the wagon and turned toward home. We were nearly out of sight when I thought I heard someone calling my name. Knowing it was probably Joshua, I plugged my ears until we were well out of hearing range. I would not let Joshua ruin my good feelings about the day. It had been wonderful to spend time with Friends again and reaffirm our beliefs. I felt good about belonging to the Society of Friends, even if it meant wearing nothing but dull gray. Maybe someday we women could help change the strict thinking of the men. And best of all, there was the prospect of a new friend. I knew no one would ever replace Maude, but one needed lots of friends, and I was anxious to get to know Betty. Even with Joshua now coming to East Grove Meeting, I felt truly happy for the first time since Father's announcement last winter.

30

**Chapter 5**

# Jezebel

A nd Ahab told Jezebel all that Elijah had done, and withal how he had slain all the prophets with the sword. Then Jezebel sent a message unto Elijah, saying, So let the gods do to me and more also, if I make not thy life as the life of one of them by tomorrow about this time.!"

Father reverently closed the family Bible after the evening's scripture reading, as quiet settled over the room. It was a Wilson family custom to share in a portion of scripture and a time of prayer when the evening meal was finished.

"Jezebel was a wicked woman, and I feel grateful the women of this family do not resemble her," Father remarked emphatically when the prayers were completed, looking at me. I was not sure if his remarks were to be taken as a compliment, or an admonition! I certainly did not feel my actions were in any way comparable to Jezebel's! I knew from the scriptures that Jezebel was a wicked, conniving woman who would stop at nothing to get what she wanted. I also knew her body was eaten by dogs outside the city's ancient walls. Just the thought of death in that manner made me shiver!

"Is thee chilled, Rebecca? Does thee feel ill?" questioned Mother anxiously.

"No, Mother, I am feeling very well. Though I suppose before too long the cabin will be too chilly for comfort and we will be enjoying the fireplace."

31

*FOR THE LOVE OF A FRIEND*

"Thee is correct, Rebecca, about the coming cooler weather," Father added. "There is much to be done if this family is to survive our first winter in Iowa."

Abigail, Jacob, Levi and I looked at each other and knew what each was thinking: more long days of work!

"We must pick the ears of corn to store in our lean-to for the new litter of pigs to eat this winter. Jacob and I will take care of that labor. Rebecca, thee, Abigail and Levi will dig the potatoes from our meager garden to store for winter. When the potatoes are dug, you will all dig a pit behind the cabin at least four feet deep, and then layer the potatoes with some of the wheat straw we have managed to save. You will then cover the hole with dirt. This should give us an adequate supply of potatoes until spring.

"Hannah, thee will need to harvest the squash and pumpkins to dry," Father said as he turned to Mother.

"I know thee has a good supply of dried fruits already stored, and these additional vegetables will provide variety for our meals." Looking again toward his children, he continued. "There will be additional work to make the cabin as secure as possible for winter, so I shall expect you to gladly lend a hand when needed. Does each of you understand thy duties?" he finally finished.

We all nodded, rather solemnly. I think in the backs of each of our minds was a bit of uneasiness about the winter months. We had been used to living in a wooden frame home that had been adequately warm in the winter, not to mention the luxury of having a general store within two blocks for any food supplies we might need. An Iowa winter, in a log cabin, was indeed a chilling prospect.

"Does thee think we will be able to make a trip into Salem for sugar, flour and coffee before the cold sets in?" Mother inquired, looking at Father.

"We will certainly need to make one trip, and I would not be surprised if we did not make several trips if the weather permits," Father replied. "I would like to take the children for

32

*Jezebel*

new shoes before the snow falls."

"Oh goodie!" Levi burst out, unable to contain his excitement. "I can't wait to go to Salem!"

"Levi, thee must learn to hold thy tongue," came Father's stern reprimand. "Getting new shoes is a necessity, and if thy feet were not the same size as Jacob's, thee would be wearing his outgrown pair. Clothing and shoes can keep one's mind on the things of the world rather than on what is pure and good."

"I'm sorry, Father," Levi was quick to seek forgiveness. Then as a second thought he added, "Does thee think we might get a penny's worth of candy there?"

Father looked at Mother and shook his head. I think he felt raising Levi in the manner of Friends was certainly going to be a challenge! Levi was a stubborn, impulsive child, but he had a tender heart and I thought Father was a little too strict with him at times!

We had acquired several additions to our "family" since our May arrival. From several members of East Grove Meeting Father was able to acquire a bit of livestock: a Jersey milk cow from the Hinshaws, and a sow nearly ready to deliver piglets from the Mendenhalls. Jacob and Father had worked many long days in August to build an open-faced shed and pen for the pigs, and a small enclosed building for the cow. It was wonderful to once again have the fresh, warm milk to sooth our stomachs, as well as the thick delicious cream on fresh berries, and butter for the bread Mother and I baked each day. It was Abigail's job to churn the butter, Jacob's job to do the milking, and my job to take the cow to fresh areas of grass each day to ensure generous milk production. I suppose Levi's job was to lick the bowls clean, for he seldom left anything uneaten!

The days were growing shorter and cooler as September was nearly over. This meant less and less time to get all the things accomplished I was asked to do each day. On one day

*FOR THE LOVE OF A FRIEND*

in particular, I was to finish digging the potatoes and it was afternoon before I completed my work in the kitchen. I had taken the cow out close to the south woods (Abigail Woods, I called them, as Abigail spent every minute she could spare playing there) early in the morning and staked her in a nice green patch which should have lasted her all day. Though we dug as fast as possible, evening was fast approaching and the task was still unfinished. Dusk would be settling soon, and I knew I would not be able to both finish the potatoes and go get the cow for milking. When Levi offered to go to the south woods for the cow, it seemed like the perfect solution to my dilema. Even though Levi was only five, he was a responsible child, and he knew how to get to south woods. Father and Mother had gone to Salem for the day to purchase supplies, so I could not ask their approval.

"Is thee sure thee knows how to get to the south woods?" I questioned, still unsure.

"Certainly, Rebecca. I have been with thee lots of times when thee took her."

"And thee will go straight to the woods and come straight back?"

"Yes, Rebecca. Thee can count on me."

"Is thee certain thee can do this job, Levi?"

"Yes, Rebecca, yes!" Levi was getting a bit exasperated with me, but I couldn't help feeling just a little apprehensive. He was only five, after all.

"All right, go. But please hurry right back," I finally consented. Levi took off running, grinning from ear to ear, proud of his newly given responsibility. I felt a little foolish for not trusting him, but I had to be careful with my responsibilities since Mother and Father would not be returning until later in the evening.

Abigail and I continued digging the hills of potatoes until the job was complete. It felt good to finally have them all unearthed, and tomorrow we would layer them in the cache behind the cabin and cover it with dirt.

*Jezebel*

It was nearly dusk when we finished, the sun's last rays faintly coloring the sky. Levi would be returning any minute with the cow, and I needed to prepare a little supper for the children. I was just slicing some bread when Jacob came in from feeding the pigs.

"Where is the cow?" he asked impatiently. "Thee should have gotten her before now! How does thee expect me to get the milking done when thee does not get the cow?!"

"Have a little patience, Jacob!" I scolded. "I sent Levi for the cow and he should be back shortly."

"It's almost dark now, Rebecca. When did thee send Levi?" he asked, his expression shifting from one of anger to worry.

"Well, let me think....now that I consider everything Abigail and I did after Levi left, it was probably about an hour ago!" I said as I began to feel weak. "Abigail and I were so busy working, the time passed very quickly."

"What are we going to do, Rebecca?" Abigail whispered, her lower lip trembling and her eyes welling with tears.

I knew I must calm their fears before I set out to look for Levi. How was I going to do that when my heart was pounding and my hands were shaking? If anything happened to my dear, sweet Levi, I would never forgive myself.

"All right, first of all we must pray," I began, doing my best to sound brave and confident. Bowing our heads, we each prayed silently for Levi's safe return.

"Thank you, Lord," I finished, as I knew we had to trust in the Lord to find Levi. It would soon be dark, and a flickering candle in a black forest would not be much help in finding a small boy and a cow.

"Now Jacob, thee and Abigail eat some bread and wild honey for thy supper. When I get home with Levi and the cow, we can have some fresh milk before bed," I said with more confidence than I felt.

Putting on a heavy woolen wrap to keep out the chilly night air, I set out for the south woods. It was just light enough

*FOR THE LOVE OF A FRIEND*

for me to see the dark outline of the trees, and I ran as fast as my legs would go. It was only a half mile, but it seemed like ten. When I reached the woods, I quickly located the spot where I had tied the cow earlier. All that remained was the broken stake and the trampled area where she had been tied.

"Levi...Levi...can thee hear me? Where art thou? Don't play games, Levi, I'm over by the broken stake. Bring the cow and come to me!" I yelled loudly, straining to hear a reply other than the dying echo of my call.

Then silence.

"Levi!" I tried again. "Where art thou? Can thee hear me?"

My only answer was a lone owl in a distant tree.

What was I to do? If I started into the forboding dark woods, I was sure to get lost. Yet I could not abandon my poor, sweet, lost Levi.

I continued to call until my hoarse voice was nearly gone. Finally, I sank to my knees and began to sob, despair filling my soul. This was the first time I had been trusted with the children's safety, and I had failed miserably. Levi might be hurt, or worse. Who knew what might happen to a small boy lost at night in the woods, all alone, and...No, I thought, this is what the devil would wish me to do. We have asked God to take care of Levi, and I must trust Him to do so.

A calming peace spread through my soul and I realized that although I could not find Levi, God could. I would have to trust Him, no matter how dark the situation appeared.

Jezebel. That was a good name for the troublesome cow. She had been a great trial for me today, and she deserved that name! I smiled as I lit my candle and began to walk along the edge of the woods which seemed less dangerous and forbidding than before. Yes, Jezebel would be my personal name for our cow. Let everyone else call her Sweet Pea!

# Chapter 6

# Good Friends

It was now completely dark as I walked the edge of the woods calling for Levi. The full moon helped light my way, for which I was grateful. Where could Levi have gone? Why hadn't he returned to the cabin when he saw the cow had broken her stake? Even more nagging was the question that kept resounding over and over in my head: why did I let Levi talk me into sending him after Jezebel? No, I knew the blame did not lie with Levi. I had wanted to get all the potatoes dug, and Levi was an easy way to accomplish my goal. I would have to take responsibility for my own poor judgment.

"Lee-vi.." I continued to call, not so much because I thought he might hear me, but simply because I didn't know what else to do. I could imagine the wrath of Father when he came home and discovered what had happened. But even that did not concern me as much as the thought of something happening to Levi.

I was nearly to the far corner of our property when I thought I heard a faint voice. Excitedly, I began to run toward the sound, stopping only when I tripped on a large tree root.

"Levi, is that thee? Call to me again...please?!" I begged desparately.

Once again there was silence. Utter despair overcame me. I was so sure I had found him...what could the sound have been?

"Rebecca....Rebecca, we are over here," came an un-

37

FOR THE LOVE OF A FRIEND

known yet familiar voice from the depths of darkness.

Quickly picking myself up off the cold, damp ground, I stumbled toward the sound. I soon reached the source-Levi, Jezebel, and John Shipling!

Running to Levi, I threw my arms around him, lifting his small chubby body off the ground in a tight embrace. "Levi, I'm so sorry," I began, now sobbing while trying to speak. "I should never have sent thee to get Jez-Sweet Pea, can thee ever forgive me?"

"I'm fine, Rebecca, don't cry. Sweet Pea broke her stake and I went after her," Levi explained patiently. Then looking a bit frightened he continued, "but it started to get dark and I couldn't see her anymore. I started to call her name, but she wouldn't come to me. I heard the creek in the distance, so I ran to it. I thought I could follow it to the cabin, but I never made it." A smile began to brightened his features as he finished his story, a story that, thankfully, had a happy ending. "Then I heard Mr. Shipling calling and he had Sweet Pea. So I DID get the cow for thee, Rebecca. I told thee I could do it!"

I hugged Levi again, holding him tightly for a moment.

Suddenly remembering we weren't the only ones in the deep woods, I turned to John. "I'm sorry for neglecting thee, John. How can I ever repay thee for saving Levi's life?"

Gentle laughter filled the air as John spoke. "I didn't save Levi, Rebecca, he saved himself. He is a very bright five-year-old. By following the creek, he was never in danger of being totally lost. It was fortunate I was working late on a fence between our lands when I first heard the cow thrashing through the brush and then before long a quieter sound, that of Levi. If Levi hadn't started walking the wrong way at the creek, he would have eventually reached your cabin."

"I did not realize thy property joined ours, John, but it certainly is a lucky thing you were still working on that fence!" I said. Then feeling a bit guilty, I ammended my words. "Actually, luck had nothing to do with it. We had prayed to God for Levi's safe return, and He answered our prayers!"

38

*Good Friends*

"You are certainly right about that, Rebecca. God always watches out for His children," came John's reply.

A warmth began to spread through me and settle in my heart as I realized John must believe in the same God Friends did. How could Father object to such a gallant, God-fearing man as John Shipling?

Resting his hand on my shoulder, John spoke once more.

"I'm just glad I was able to help, Rebecca," he reassured me with a tender smile. Then turning to Levi, he continued, "You are lucky to have a big sister to care about you, Levi. She is a pretty special woman!" he finished, looking back at me.

My heart began to beat a little faster! John thought I was special! He really had noticed me, and I felt like jumping for joy! Of course, I didn't, because about that time I heard a loud, booming voice echoing through the woods. "Rebecca...Levi? Where art thou?" came Father's cry.

"We're over here, Mr. Wilson," John responded quickly, "To your left."

Soon Father was grabbing Levi and looking reproachfully at me. "What was thee thinking, Rebecca? Sending a five year old in the dark to fetch an old milk cow? Thee knows better!"

"I'm sorry, Father," I began lamely, "it wasn't dark when he left and..."

"We will discuss this further, thee can be sure, when we return to the cabin!" Father interrupted sternly. Turning to John, he continued. "Am I to suppose it was thee who found Levi, John?"

"I was working on the fence when I heard the cow and Levi, and I was just helping them get back home. Rebecca was also searching and found them nearly the same time I did. She should receive as much credit as I for their rescue."

I could feel myself blush just a bit as John stretched the truth to try and ease the tension between Father and me. Being totally honest was something Friends were well known for, and it always bothered me when untruths were knowingly spoken. In this case, however, John was trying to be a friend,

39

*FOR THE LOVE OF A FRIEND*

and I could surely admire him for that.

"I am still grateful to thee for thy part in their safe return," Father said to John, "and I hope we will never have a repeat of tonight's folly. Rebecca," he continued, turning to me, "we must not keep the others waiting. They are worried enough as it is. Get the cow, and we will be on our way. Farewell, John. Perhaps I can help thee with thy fence tomorrow to repay thy kindness to my family."

"That is not necessary, Mr. Wilson. I am nearly finished."

"Please call me Alfred, John, after the manner of Friends. We are all equal in God's eyes."

"All right, Alfred," John replied. As Father turned to go, John turned to me and in a soft voice continued, "It was nice to see you again, Rebecca. Perhaps next time we meet it will be under better circumstances!"

Not knowing how to reply, I simply smiled and began walking behind Father, who was carrying Levi. This had been a day of great turmoil, but there had been a silver lining in the cloud, and now I had something to look forward to—seeing John Shipling again!


Father must have known my deep regret at having sent Levi after Jezebel, for he did not speak to me again of the foolishness of my actions. Mother had been amazingly calm when we returned, not even shedding a tear! She told us how she had prayed for the safe return of us all, and how God had given her a calm assurance He would do just that. I knew Mother had a strong faith, but it was never clearer to me than at that moment.

Abigail and Jacob were not quite as calm, and both wanted to hug Levi, even though he was now fast asleep on Father's shoulder. I volunteered to get Levi ready for bed and suprisingly, Mother quickly agreed. I sensed she knew the agony I had experienced when I had not been able to find Levi, and this was her way of letting me know all was forgiven. I

40

*Good Friends*

hoped when I had children of my own I would be as under-standing as Mother had been tonight.


Mother continued to treat me with kindness in the days that followed, and I tried to respond in ways that let her know I appreciated that kindness. I did extra chores around the cabin, even volunteering to chink some of the holes which had appeared over the months as the original mud and grass dried and crumbled.

On the day I finished that unpleasant task, Mother com-pletely suprised me by asking if I would like to go with her and Abigail to the Jessops the next day. They were going to butcher a hog, and Mother would help Mrs. Jessop with the sausage making.

Would I like to go?! I would love to go! Even though hog butchering seemed cruel when I thought of our own plump little piglets, I knew the pork would be a wonderful addition to the Jessops' winter food supply.

I was ready to go as soon as breakfast was over, but Mother thought we needed to fix food to leave for Father and the boys. Although I kept quiet, I didn't understand why they couldn't fix something to eat themselves! We women were expected to do some of the outside chores, yet the men rarely made themselves useful in the cabin.

"I will expect thee to be on thy best behavior," Mother reminded Abigail as we were in the wagon and on our way. Then looking at me, she continued, "I am not bringing thee to relax and play, Rebecca. Thee will be expected to help with the butchering."

Abigail and I were too excited about the trip to even answer. We had had very little chance to spend time with other girls our age, and we couldn't wait. I had not seen Betty Jessop since the monthly meeting picnic, except to greet her at meeting each Sabbath. I knew she had a younger sister almost Abigail's age, so we would not have to worry about a tag-along sister listening to our conversations! It was going to be a great day!

The men were just plunging the squealing hog into a barrel of boiling water when we arrived. It looked like one of the other families from our meeting had come to help them butcher as well as Mother, Abigail and me. I must admit the odor of the scalding hog was almost more than I could bear. I felt my stomach begin to churn the breakfast I had eaten earlier, and I quickly turned away in search of Betty.

As soon as Betty saw me looking rather pale, she came running, reaching for my hand to pull me toward the cabin. "Rebecca, what is thee doing standing by that awful hog smell?" Betty inquired. "Come into the kitchen with me and we can help Mother prepare for the hog. The men will need to scrape the skin before they remove it, and then they will do the cutting, so we might even have a little time to ourselves before working with the sausage!" she finished excitedly.

We quickly ran into the cabin. The Jessop's cabin was quite similar to ours, the exception being the room they had built onto the back for sleeping. Betty and her sister slept in the loft just as we children did, and as soon as everything was ready in the kitchen we climbed the ladder to her room.

"I know I probably shouldn't ask this of thee;" I began when we were sitting on her mattress, "but I was wondering if thee would mind telling me thy age?!"

"How old does thee think I am?" Betty asked with that now familiar twinkle in her eye.

"Well, I was hoping thee was near my age-fifteen."

"Actually, I am seventeen, but I prefer not to tell everyone, especially since I do not have any young men asking Father's permission to come courting!" was Betty's honest reply. "There are many days when I don't care if I ever get married, but neither do I want to live with Mother and Father forever!"

"I can certainly understand thy feelings. Sometimes I think men are so offensive, like Joshua Frazier, for instance. He can irritate me quicker than anyone I know!"

*Good Friends*

Smiling a little, Betty's next words were a complete shock. "I think Joshua is rather good looking—in a boyish sort of way. His family visits with ours nearly every week, but when I try to talk to him, he just seems to ignore me!"

"That sounds just like Joshua," I burst in. "He only thinks of himself, if you ask me!"

Knowing it was unlikely we would agree on the subject of Joshua, and since he wasn't really a topic I enjoyed discussing, I quickly asked another question to change the subject.

"Betty, does thee think Friends have the right way to worship God? With all the silence, I mean, and no minister?"

Pausing as she contemplated how to best answer my question, Betty finally began a message to me that I would remember long into adulthood. She said, "Rebecca, I do not know if Friends have all the right answers in regard to worship and custom. I do believe if one is comfortable with the way she worships, God will speak individually to his children no matter how they choose to try and listen; whether it be through the Holy Spirit in the silence, or by spoken word from a minister, or through gathering together in groups of two or three to pray. I am comfortable with Friends' beliefs. I believe George Fox was wise to believe we should strive to be a peculiar people, not like others who proclaim to love God, but have no actions to show that love. Our use of "thee" and "thou", like the Lord used when he addressed a servant, makes sense to me, as does the plain clothing we choose to wear. But you, Rebecca, have to decide what is best for you, and in what manner you can best worship and serve our risen Savior."

I wasn't sure how to respond to her poignant words, but I sensed I had just received a message from God through my new friend, Betty Jessop. I did resolve to try and center down more in meeting and hear what God had to say to me.

Just then Betty's mother called up to let us know it was time to help with the sausage stuffing. Since this would probably be our last chance to be alone, I squeezed Betty's hand to let her know how much her words had meant to me.

*FOR THE LOVE OF A FRIEND*

"Betty, if Friends ever have ministers, thee should consider becoming one!" I couldn't help but say.

"Thee is a wonderful friend, Rebecca. I will remember thy kind words. However, I think perhaps God has something else in mind for me to do at this point in my life," Betty finished with a secretive smile.

"What is it?" I demanded, now really curious as to what she had meant.

"Betty...Rebecca, we need thee now!" came Mrs. Jessop's voice again.

"We'd better get down there and help," Betty said as she scrambled for the ladder. We will talk again soon."

I hoped Betty and I would have many more conversations as we got to know each other better. Little did I know how soon my wish would come true!

**Chapter 7**

# Education

"R ebecca! Rebecca!" Abigail shouted excitedly as she threw open the cabin door one early fall day in October. "Thee will never guess what I just heard Father say!"

I knew there was only one thing that could cause such great excitement to be reflected in the shining eyes of Abigail's radiant face: something to do with school. I knew Abigail greatly missed the Richmond Public Library that she and I had visited so many times, not to mention the challenge of getting good marks in school. Not wanting to spoil her great surprise, however, I pretended I had no idea what her news could be.

"Well, thee might as well tell me before thee uses all thy energy jumping up and down!" I teased her.

"Rebecca, I heard Father talking to Clyde Jessop just now. Clyde rode over on his horse," she added as an after thought, in case I wondered how he had gotten here!"Anyway, Mr. Jessop told Father the elders were going to gather in a special meeting after Sabbath meeting tomorrow to discuss starting a school! Isn't that just the most wonderful news?! I can't wait! New books to read! Figuring to do! Stories to write! Isn't it wonderful, Rebecca?!" she exclaimed, hugging me and dancing up and down.

Gently smiling, I replied, "Yes, Abigail, that is great news for thee. I imagine Jacob will not be as thrilled as thee, but Levi should share thy excitement as this will be his first

45

*FOR THE LOVE OF A FRIEND*

opportunity to have formal lessons."

"What about thee, Rebecca? Isn't thee happy, too, about starting a school?" she asked expectantly.

Trying not to let my disappointment spoil her excitement, I reluctantly told her that when children reached my age, they were often expected to end their formal education, unless they could afford to board at a high school. Since there was no opportunity for me to do that in the Iowa territory, I would probably remain at home with Mother to help with sewing and cooking.

"That's not fair!" cried Abigail indignantly. "Thee doesn't know everything there is to know! Thee needs to go to school too!"

Laughing at her eight-year-old wisdom, I said with as much enthusiasm as I could possibly muster, "I will still get to help thee learn thy lessons at night, and maybe I WILL learn new things!"

I hated to admit it to anyone, but I was going to miss school this year. Of course, Father had not actually said I would no longer be attending school, but I knew of too many instances where the older children had to let the younger ones have their places as they stayed home to help their parents. I would have to be content to help my siblings with their lessons. Perhaps we would soon have a library in Salem, and I would be able to continue my education on my own.

Later that evening, after our family time together, Father confirmed Abigail's earlier announcement.

"I imagine East Grove Friends will want to begin a school soon. Clyde knows of a cabin that has been abandoned near the meeting house that he believes we can acquire the use of for a small fee. We will be meeting after worship tomorrow to discuss the possibility."

Remembering our earlier conversation, Abigail quickly asked Father the question I was too afraid to ask. "Father, Rebecca will be able to attend this year, won't she? She can still learn new things!"

46

*Education*

This brought a slight smile to Father's usually stern countenance as he shifted his gaze my way. Although his reply was addressed to Abigail, I knew his words were meant for me. "There are many details yet to work out , Abigail. We will know more after tomorrow. Now thee had all best get to bed so thy bodies will be prepared for the Sabbath."

There was hope! Maybe just a faint glimmer, but Father had not said I couldn't go to school. But he hadn't said I could, either, I had to remind myself. I would have to pray tonight as I had never prayed before that God might find it in His will to allow me to attend school this year. I loved Mother dearly, but the thought of staying home and working while the others were off learning new and exciting things was just about more than I could bear!

I had a particularly hard time quieting my heart and mind during worship the next day. It seemed that the harder I tried, the more thoughts of school crowded in. I even forgot to stand once when another woman rose to pray, and Mother had to reach down and pull me up! That was certainly embarrasing!

While the elders met to discuss the school after worship, Betty and I escaped to her family's wagon for a visit. The October air was crisp and cool, but the sun was shining brightly, and I was too busy thinking about the school to be cold, anyway! Then it hit me like a thunderbolt: Betty was seventeen, and there was not even a possibility she could attend. I felt guilty for my own excitement, and tried to be sympathetic to her concerns.

"Does thee think they will buy the cabin and start a school soon, Betty?" I couldn't help but ask.

"Oh, I'm quite certain they will, Rebecca. Father has talked to the elders, and they are all in favor. Thee knows how important education is to Friends! Father says they will probably build a larger school some time next spring, but for now the cabin will be sufficient. They are probably discussing

*FOR THE LOVE OF A FRIEND*

some of the details of running the school in today's meeting. For instance, I'm certain selecting a teacher will be one of their considerations."

"I hadn't even thought of that! Do they have someone in mind? Someone who has taught before, I mean?"

"Well," Betty began rather slowly, "I think they may have someone in mind, but I'm not free to say who it might be."

I was a little hurt that Betty didn't feel she could trust me, but I did not want to make an issue of it. We continued to chat about our sausage stuffing experience, (both of us decided we could live without sausage!) and what we had been doing since we were last together.

"Hey girls!" called an all too familiar voice! "Why don't you come and play tag with the rest of us?" came Joshua's request.

"Tag is for children!" I said rather scornfully. "We have more important things to do!"

"Like what? You are becoming just like two old maids! You are no fun at all!" he replied disgustedly.

"We could have joined the fun for a short time," Betty said quietly when Joshua had gone to resume playing with the others.

"Betty, thee can play games with Joshua if thee wishes, but I will not go near him! And furthermore, in the future I would appreciate it if thee would not mention his name in my presence!"

"All right, Rebecca. But I think thee is wrong to dislike Joshua so. He is one of God's children, just as we are, and thy anger toward him is not very God-like," she chided gently.

I looked away so Betty could not glimpse the deep hurt in my eyes. I had thought she would understand my feelings, but instead she had chosen to defend Joshua! Even if there was some truth to her words, I was not ready or willing to admit it.

When the elders' meeting was over, everyone was gathered in front of the meeting house. As the Presiding Clerk of the monthly meeting, Clyde Jessop spoke to the Friends.

48

*Education*

"There has been a consensus among the elders on the matter of beginning a school in the East Grove Community. We will purchase the abandoned cabin which sits a mile west of the meeting house to use for the education of our children. We have chosen a teacher from among those showing an interest in the position. My daughter, Elizabeth, has gotten high marks in all subjects during her previous school attendance, and she has a great love for children. Her knowledge of the Word of God and Friend's beliefs, combined with her love for God will insure a continuation of our doctrine to the next generation. The elders feel she will be able to educate all children in the meeting in a manner which we will approve.

"Each family will support the school as they feel best able. Most importantly, we need each of you to loan whatever books you might have brought from Indiana to share with the others. Children will be expected to bring wood for the fire each day, and I will see that Elizabeth is there early to get the cabin warm before school begins.

"Are there any concerns Friends wish to speak to?" Clyde asked.

James Mendenhall was the only one to speak, but he asked the question to which I so desparately wanted an answer. "Will there be any age limit for attendance?"

Clyde was slow and careful to reply, as he knew there were several children present who would be affected by his answer. "Of course," he began, "we would like to provide an opportunity for any child who wishes to attend for learning. The cabin, however, is quite small. There are twenty children in our meeting under the age of fourteen and over the age of five that may attend. If they all choose to do so, that will be all the building can hold."

I could not help the tears of disappointment that began to well up in my eyes and slip down my cheeks. It was so unfair! I knew there were children who would rather stay home and work than go to school, like Jacob for instance. Jacob would probably till the soil for a living like Father, so why did he need

49

*FOR THE LOVE OF A FRIEND*

an education, especially when he didn't want one? Why couldn't I go in his place? I knew the answer to the question before I even asked, but it still seemed unfair to me.

Putting her arm around my shoulder, Betty's kind words, "I'm sorry Rebecca," helped ease my pain. Her next words were a puzzlement to me, however. "Thee knows that sometimes things work for the best even when they look the darkest."

"That's easy for thee to say," I retorted angrily, not even trying to hide my disappointment. "Thee gets the best job in the world, and I get to sew and cook at home!" I knew my words were bitter, but I had prayed so hard I was certain God would answer my prayer.

"I'm so sorry," Betty said again, and I knew she meant it.

Realizing how selfish I must have sounded, I swallowed my tears and heartache and turned to give her a hug. "Thee will be a great teacher, Betty. Thee has already taught me a lot in the short time I have known thee. I know Abigail, Jacob and Levi will learn a lot from thee, and I will do my best to help them learn their lessons," I finally managed to say.

"Has thee ever thought about teaching, Rebecca?" Betty asked suddenly. "Thee knows a great deal about many things, and I believe thee would be good with the children."

"No, I have never really thought of being a teacher. Of course, I was always a student until this year. I do like to help the others with their lessons, so I suppose I could do a good job. Perhaps there will be another meeting nearby that needs a teacher, although I doubt they would want to trust the education of their children to a fifteen year old!" I finished sadly with a look of defeat.

"I have an idea that just might work!" Betty began, her voice cautiously excited.

"What is it?" I asked, curiously.

"I can't really tell thee now, in case it doesn't work out. But I promise to let thee know as soon as I get an answer. Thee will have to trust me!"

*Education*

This was the second time today Betty had asked me to trust her. From the look on her face, I knew it was useless to ask again about her idea. She did have my interest, though. What could she be thinking of? A tutor, perhaps? Or maybe she knew of a school that needed a teacher, but she didn't want to get my hopes up. Whatever it was, I couldn't wait for her to share the idea as well as the part I might play in it.

"I will ask Father if I may ride the horse to thy home as soon as I have the answer. It should be within a few days. Will that be all right with thee?" Betty asked expectantly.

"I don't even know the question, let alone the answer!" I said as a smile found its way to my solemn face. "But I know I will have a hard time concentrating on my tasks this week until I see thee coming!" Betty's gentle laughter warmed my heart, and suddenly things looked brighter.

As all Friends' hearts and minds were at ease in regard to the new school, we said our farewells and were soon heading our separate ways, with plenty to think about and look forward to. What could Betty possibly have in mind for me? Once again it seemed I was anxiously awaiting the future, and I knew there would be some sleepless nights as I thought of all the possibilities!

## Chapter 8

# Surprise Visitor

C hildren," Father began as we were just finishing our meal
    one early October morning, "as you will soon be
walking nearly two miles to school, I believe we shall travel
to Salem tomorrow to purchase new shoes. Your mother
wishes to purchase heavier cloth for our winter garments and
I have several items of business to attend to as well, so I
imagine we will be gone for most of the day. We will take our
dinner with us and leave immediately following morning
chores."

There were excited grins on four faces that morning as we
anticipated the next day's adventure. It would be the first time
we children had been to Salem since our arrival in May, and
I, for one, was anxious to see if there were any new additions
to the town. The possibility of a new library, however slim it
was, gave me a fresh and new excitement that helped ease the
pain of the preceding day's school announcement. I still could
not imagine what Betty's idea was, but a trip to town would
help keep my mind occupied while I anxiously waited.

As soon as breakfast was finished the next morning,
Mother and I made plans for all the purchases we would need
for the cabin to insure our survival through the long winter
months. Food staples were always a necessity, but we now
had school supplies to consider as well. Father had decided
the three younger children would need slates for their math

*FOR THE LOVE OF A FRIEND*

figuring, as well as some type of container for their lunches. We had taken these simple things for granted in Richmond, but careful planning was needed here in East Grove where the nearest store was five miles from home instead of just down the street.

"Mother," I asked cautiously as we finished writing our list, unsure of how to phrase the question on my mind, "Does thee believe God chooses one's husband? Or are we expected to use our God-given minds to select the mate we feel would best suit our needs?"

I fixed my gaze on the table as I was too embarrassed to look at Mother for her answer, but certain I would have seen a smile had I been able to look. "Rebecca," she slowly began to answer, "Friends believe that God has a perfect plan for each of our lives. We must be in close communication with God so as to hear His voice and thus know His will for us. The Inner Light of God within each of us will confirm that perfect will. If we use only our minds to try and determine God's plan, we often fail because human thinking is determined by the things of this world, not the things of God." Pausing a moment, as if trying to decide whether or not to continue, she hesitantly asked, "Does thee have an idea of God's will for thee with regard to thy future husband?"

"Oh no!" I quickly replied. "I was thinking more of Betty than myself! Betty is seventeen and as no one has asked her father's permission to court her, I was just wondering whether she should be seeking God's will in the matter." I wasn't being totally honest—in the manner of Friends—but I just couldn't admit to Mother that thoughts of a husband had been on my mind!

"I would not be too concerned about Betty, Rebecca. She is a lovely girl who loves the Lord a great deal. With her new teaching position, she will no doubt find her days too full to be concerned with seeking a husband for some time!" Mother finished with the smile I was sure had been there all along. "Now, if we don't finish fixing our dinner, we won't be ready

54

*Surprise Visitor*

when Father and the others finish chores, so we had best hurry with our preparations!"

Knowing this discussion was finished, I began to think about mother's words as I prepared the potatoes and sausage given to us by the Jessops for our lunch. Perhaps I had not heard the words from Mother I had hoped to hear, but at least she had not said God intended for Friends to marry only other Friends. I did not think I wanted to ask Father's opinion on the subject, as I was rather certain of his answer, an answer that would not include a certain young man by the name of John Shipling!

A warm feeling spread through my body as I thought of all the wonderful opportunities that might lie ahead! Packing the last of the sausages, I determined to seek God's will for my life, in particular for that husband He might have for me!

The slow five mile journey to Salem seemed like at least ten! Every time we would turn on a different path, Levi would ask if we were there yet! Father's patience was wearing thin, and Mother finally looked back at me wearily as if to say, "Please keep thy brother quiet!"

I did my best to keep the others entertained. We talked mostly of school subjects, as well as what we might see when we got to Salem. When we finally pulled into the town, it was past noon. None of us children felt hungry, but Father insisted we have our dinner before taking care of our business. He didn't want us to become hungry before the purchases were made and business transacted. It was probably the fastest dinner ever eaten; even Father and Mother were finished in a hurry!

Our first order of business was purchasing the new shoes. The younger children were first, then Jacob and me. There was no problem in selecting a style; there was only one style! The store owner did, however, have a pair of black patent leather boots in the store window. They were the most beau-

55

*FOR THE LOVE OF A FRIEND*

tiful boots I had ever seen, but I knew better than to ask to try them on, no matter how badly I wanted them. In fact, there was certain to be a long sermon from Father right where we stood if he even saw me looking at them! In spite of the possiblilty of a lecture, it was still difficult to keep from thinking how nice they might look on my feet!

When we had the matter of the shoes taken care of, Father suggested I take the children to the large yard behind the Salem Meeting House to let them run off some of their energy. Actually, I think he was hoping they would wear themselves out playing and then fall asleep on the way home. That way Levi could not ask him over and over if we were almost there! Father and Mother would each complete their business in town and then we would start for home.

"Could we walk up and down the street before we go?" I asked cautiously. "Just to see what the town looks like?" I knew Levi and Abigail were having a hard time keeping their eyes, not to mention their fingers, away from the tantilizing candy sitting on the counter. I was hoping this would occupy their minds for awhile.

"If thee will be responsible for thy brothers and sister," Father said as he looked to make sure I knew he was referring to the near tragedy of the lost cow, "thee may walk once down each side of the street to see the town."

"Thank you Father. I will take good care of them!"

"Thee will need to keep an eye on the wagon," he warned, "so thee will know when we are ready to return and can bring the children. We will leave it in front of the general store."

We had difficulty keeping our feet from carrying us faster than a walking pace! It was such fun to explore the town. There were several new businesses including a millinery and doctor's office, but not surprisingly, no library. It did not take long to walk up and down the dusty main street, and we were soon back at the open field.

"Why don't you children play a game of tag," I suggested, "and I will sit under that far tree to watch the wagon."

*Surprise Visitor*

Levi was declared "it", and the game was soon under way. Sitting with the lulling warmth of the afternoon sun on my back, I was soon having difficulty staying awake as the previous night's lack of sleep began to catch up with me. Just as my head started to nod, I was jolted awake by a deep male voice calling my name.

"Rebecca? Is that you?" came the inquiry.

"John! John Shipling! What...what is thee doing in Salem?" I stammered drowsily, experiencing pleasure at seeing his smiling face.

"Hello, Rebecca! I thought that was Levi I saw when Father and I drove into Salem. We came for winter supplies and for a new horse. I took a chance that you might be near Levi when I walked over here. Would you mind if I sat and talked for just a while?" he asked expectantly.

"No, no, of course not! We came to Salem today to purchase shoes and supplies and I am helping the children release some of their energy! We are going to have a school near East Grove soon, and we needed school supplies, and Mother needed staples as well. Father had some business at the bank and the blacksmith, so we came here." I stopped suddenly, realizing I was babbling on like a loose-tongued fool!

"I'm sorry, John, to carry on so! Thee must forgive me!" I tried to apologize, feeling my cheeks flush as the blood rushed to my face.

Flashing that shining smile I liked so much, John quickly eased my embarrassment. "I like to listen to you talk, Rebecca. You have a lovely voice, and besides, I am anxious to know about the school. I had heard the Friends were planning to begin one, and I was curious to know more about it. Do you plan to attend?"

"No, I am much too old to attend primary school!" I said lightly, trying to act older than my fifteen and a half years. "Does thee know Betty Jessop? She is going to be the teacher," I added, hoping to change the subject.

*FOR THE LOVE OF A FRIEND*

"I have met Clyde Jessop, but I am not acquainted with his family. I should think you would make a good teacher, Rebecca. Were you interested in the position?"

Not wanting John to know that less than forty-eight hours earlier I had been in tears because I could not be a student, I tried to sound as if I had given the idea some consideration.

"I have thought about being a teacher, but I'm not certain if I am ready to assume the responsibility for the education of others' children. Thee is kind to believe I would be a good teacher!" I added warmly.

"Rebecca," John paused, as if not knowing quite how to say what was on his mind, "do you think your father might consider allowing me to visit your home occasionally? I would ask his permission, of course, but I thought you might know whether or not he would allow you to see a member of the Mormon faith," he finished uneasily.

This was such a surprise request, I did not know how to respond! John Shipling wanted to come to see me! At my home! Surely Father could not object to such a polite, considerate, young man! At least, that was my opinion of him! Of course, it was not my opinion that mattered—it was Father's. Why did I have a such a sinking feeling in my heart when I thought of Father's likely response to John's calling?

"I don't know, John," I finally said, trying to be as honest as I could without hurting him or saying something that might cause him to believe I didn't want him to come calling. "I can speak to him about the subject of Quakers and Mormons, without actually mentioning thy name. If he seems receptive, then thee could formally ask to call. But how would I let thee know?"

Thinking for a moment, John suddenly seemed to come up with an idea. "Would you be able to meet me at the place where we found Levi and the cow? We could plan a day to meet, and if you don't arrive, I'll assume your father was not receptive to my faith—nor to me."

"I'm sure Father likes thee, John!" I hastily answered,

58

*Surprise Visitor*

trying to reassure him. "If thee will tell me the day and hour, I will try to have a reply for thee."

"Very well, would Friday, around ten in the morning give you enough time?" John asked, hopefully.

"Yes, that should be sufficient time for me to seek Father's feelings on the matter." I wanted to tell him how much I hoped Father would be receptive; how glad I was to see him; how much I wanted him to come calling. But not wanting him to think I was too forward, I simply smiled and tried to think of a new topic of discussion.

John must have been thinking the same thing, because he quickly asked about the school, the children, our purchases, and the return journey. Just as I was about to tell him about Levi, and Father's hope that he would be too tired to ask the same questions over and over on the way home, the sound of Father clearing his throat made us turn as his stern voice interrupted.

"Rebecca, did I not ask thee to watch the wagon and be ready to bring the children for our return home? Mother and I have been waiting for a number of minutes for thee, and I finally came to see if there was a problem," he finished, looking rather disturbed at John.

"I'm sorry, Alfred," John was quick to jump up and apologize. "Father and I came for supplies and I saw Levi playing. I was wondering how he survived his ordeal in the woods, so I came to inquire of Rebecca. She was kind enough to answer my questions about the school you are starting. Please accept my apology for keeping you waiting."

Father stared at John for a long time, as if trying to decide if there were more to the story. Finally turning to me he said sharply, "Get the others, Rebecca, and start for the wagon. I will be there shortly."

Knowing better than to say anything, I quickly gathered the children and took them to the wagon where Mother was waiting.

"Where has thee been, Rebecca? Thy father wanted to

*FOR THE LOVE OF A FRIEND*

leave quite some time ago! Thee knows how he feels about responsibility!"

"I'm sorry, Mother, I really am. Does thee remember the young man who helped find Levi the night thee and Father were in Salem? John Shipling?" I asked.

"Yes," Mother replied wonderingly with a strange look in her eyes. "He also helped with the cabin raising, did he not?"

"Yes, he did. When he and his father rode into Salem, he saw Levi playing and he wanted to see how he was after being lost in the woods. We began discussing the new school, among other things, and I forgot to watch for Father. Will thee forgive me?" I added, as I glanced back in the direction I knew Father and John were. I was growing more and more apprehensive as to what they could be discussing all this time. John would surely not ask Father if he could come calling before I had a chance to talk to him about the Mormons!

Mother saw my concerned glance, and remained silent. I knew she was trying to put all the pieces together in this new puzzle, and from the look on her face, I did not think I would like the picture she was forming in her mind!

When Father finally climbed on the wagon, my heart was pounding and I was clutching the hard side of the wagon so tightly my knuckles were white. Father remained silent for nearly a mile out of town, and I was feeling a tiny bit of relief. Perhaps he and John had simply been talking about farming, or some other common topic.

I jumped nervously when Father finally spoke.

"Rebecca, thee and I will have a long talk when we have arrived home and finished the evening chores. Thee is becoming a woman, and there is much thee needs to know. Perhaps I should have spoken to thee sooner, but I had no idea it was necessary. I still think of thee as a child, and I suppose the time has come to put the childish things behind."

Father had spoken, and there was no need for me to reply. What did he need to say to me? Would he tell me there would be no visits from John? Perhaps he did not even realize I had

*Surprise Visitor*

an interest in him. In that case, then what would he have to speak to me about?

I could now relate to Levi and his constant questioning as I longed to ask over and over again when we would arrive home. Levi had done as Father suspected: fallen fast asleep within a few yards of Salem. I wished I were as lucky! I knew Christians were not to worry, but this time I thought I had something worth taking the time to worry about! Before the evening was over, I would know if there could be any future with John Shipling!

# Chapter 9

# Treasure Hunter

Jacob, thee will feed and milk the cow while I take care of the hogs," Father commanded when we finally reached our cabin. Now nearly dark, the buildings cast eerie shadows which matched the dark uncertainty in my soul.

"Rebecca, would thee please wake Abigail and help her prepare for bed? If she is too sleepy for our time of reading God's Word and prayer, you may put her to bed with Levi."

Gently waking Abigail, I helped her down from the wagon. Her long cornsilk braids repeatedly tickled my face as I tried to steer her toward the dimly lit cabin. When we finally made it through the door, I knew it would be impossible for her to stay awake for our family time. Getting her up the ladder was a struggle, but we finally reached the top rung and nearly fell onto the floor of the loft. As I tucked her into bed, she began to wake a bit with a sleepy smile. "I like John Shipling, Rebecca. He said he might come visit us some day. Wouldn't that be nice?" she said to herself, as much as to me, before she drifted back to sleep.

"Yes, that would be nice," I whispered to myself, hoping with all my heart her words would be prophetic.

When Levi was also tucked in, I returned to the kitchen to help Mother unpack the remains of our picnic dinner. It occured to me that the younger children had not had any supper, but I supposed the sticks of peppermint candy Father

63

had surprised them with from the General Store would probably keep them full until breakfast. Remembering the excitement shining in Levi's eyes when Father had handed him the candy sack on the way home, I was determined to provide as many unexpected pleasures as possible for my own children some day. I did not mind our simple lifestyle, but neither did I see any harm in having joyous surprises now and then to lift our spirits.

When we all had finished our tasks, Father, Mother, Jacob and I sat down to eat a thick slice of bread and butter and a warm, foamy glass of milk. The sweet candy Levi had shared was certainly a treat, but it could not compare with the wholesome goodness of bread and milk.

When our small meal was finished, Father seemed to search an extra long time for the scripture he wished to share. As he slowly began reading, I wondered why he had chosen those particular verses until he read the last few: "Be ye not unequally yoked together with unbelievers; for what fellowship hath righteousness with unrighteousness and what communion hath light with darkness? Wherefore come out from among them, and be ye separate, saith the Lord, and touch not the unclean thing; and I will receive you. Second Corinthians chapter six."

Slowly looking toward me he asked, "What does thee believe to be the meaning of these verses, Rebecca?"

I was not sure how to answer, as I was not accustomed to Father asking me to share my beliefs.

Maybe Father did not expect me to reply, however, because he soon continued. "Does thee believe Christians can be yoked, or married, to nonbelievers?"

Knowing he was referring to John, I felt it was time for me to speak.

"I know John Shipling believes in God!" I replied defensively.

"Thee knows the scriptures say even the heathen believe there is a God, Rebecca. But does thee know what the

*Treasure Hunter*

Mormons believe about God?"

"No, I suppose I am not familiar with their particular beliefs," I admitted reluctantly. I knew I was about to be given a history lesson on the Mormon faith, but I also knew I needed to know more before I could sense Father's opinion as well as ease my mind about John.

Looking at Jacob, as if suddenly just remembering he was still at the table, Father quickly said, "Jacob, thee may go to bed now as we were up early this morning for chores."

As soon as Jacob climbed the ladder to the portion of the loft he and Levi shared, Father began again.

"The Mormon faith had its beginnings in the person of Joseph Smith, whose father was also named Joseph Smith. Although many Mormons today feel the younger Smith was a great prophet, history will show that he was little more than a seeker of treasure, one who was addicted to using a peek stone to find lost objects, digging throughout the area in New York where his family lived.

"Now, young Joseph claimed to have a heavenly vision one day, in which an angel by the name of Moroni, the glorified son of Mormon, appeared to him. Moroni told him where he was to dig and find a set of golden plates, which Joseph claims to have done. He then supposedly proceeded to translate these plates into English. Naturally, no one ever saw the plates, and there has never been any proof of their existence. Joseph then suggested he had been visited by John the Baptist, who conferred the Aaronic Priesthood upon him. Following this so-called miraculous event, Joseph, his brothers, and a few followers founded a new religious society known as The Church of Jesus Christ Latter Day Saints—called Mormons for short, in reference to the angel Moroni. The translation of the plates became the Book of Mormon which these followers believe belongs with our Holy Scriptures. There is more to the story, but this is the foundation of the religion." Father paused as though seeking to know my response to his words.

*FOR THE LOVE OF A FRIEND*

When I didn't speak, he continued. "One of the peculiar beliefs many Mormons hold is that of polygomy—one man marrying many women during his life on earth. It is largely because of that particular aspect of the faith that there are many members now living in Iowa and states further west, having been driven from their homes for practicing this polygomy. Joseph Smith himself was killed by a mob who did not appreciate his influence in their community of Nauvoo.

"Rebecca, does thee believe this doctrine and faith, based on the unproven words of a greedy treasure hunter, is in agreement with Friends' beliefs? Does thee believe a Friend and a Mormon could ever be equally yoked in marriage? And would thee be willing to share thy husband with other women?" Father's voice was quiet and gentle, and I knew he was trying to enlarge my understanding while saving my pride. I wasn't sure that was possible.

"But Father, John believes in God—he even said so!" I reminded him hopefully.

"Rebecca, if thee were to read the Book of Mormon, thee would find references to many Gods. Thee knows the scriptures clearly say there is only one God Almighty. Which God does John worship?"

All hope of Father's approval of John was gone. If Father was telling me the truth, which of course I knew he was, it would be impossible for a Friend to marry a Mormon. I felt as if a crushing blow had been dealt me, and I could not speak.

"Rebecca," Father continued gently, "Friends also believe they must marry within the faith to maintain the integrity of our calling. If thee were to marry someone of any other faith, thee would be cut off from the meeting. And Mother and I as well," he added. "Thee is only fifteen with many years to discover the man God has chosen for thee."

I made one last attempt to change Father's mind. "Perhaps John could be convinced to become a Friend. I know his father does not practice polygomy, so perhaps his faith is not so strong. He seems like such a wise person, I'm sure if thee were

66

to tell him the things thee has told me, he would know the Mormon faith was not the will of God!" I was nearly pleading now, so badly did I want Father to approve of John.

"Rebecca, we are to be separate, touching not the unclean thing. We must let John and his father associate with the other Mormons nearby, and we will only associate with Friends." Father's words were firm and final. "When I spoke with John in the park, I told him what I have just told thee. He knows there will be no association between the two of you. Now it is getting late, and thee needs to go to thy bed."

Father rose, and I knew there would be no more discussion tonight—or ever—where John Shipling was concerned.

Climbing the ladder, I couldn't help the hot tears which fell silently on the now smooth rungs of the ladder. I had had such high hopes only a few hours ago, and now they were completely gone. If Friends were to marry only other Friends, where was I ever to find a suitable husband? The boys close to my age in meeting were childish, especially Joshua Frazier. There were no Quarterly Meetings here in Iowa as there had been in Indiana, which meant no other opportunities to meet eligible men!

Lying in bed, unable to sleep, I wrestled over and over with the hopeless situation. Why couldn't John become a Friend? I knew believers were to spread the gospel to others, so why did Father forbid me to even see John?

Then another thought occurred to me...would John still keep our meeting arrangement on Friday? Would I dare try to meet him? If Father caught me there, I knew the punishment would be severe. Was it worth the risk? I so wanted to see John and explain my true feelings. I was sure Father had been less than pleasant with him this afternoon.

I knew I should pray about going, but for some reason I couldn't. Maybe I was angry with God, maybe just afraid to ask for fear of the answer He might give.

I finally drifted into a restless, dreamless sleep as the first streaks of dawn appeared in the east .

*FOR THE LOVE OF A FRIEND*

"Rebecca," Mother began as we were attacking the mending Friday morning, "I'm sorry thee has been so troubled this week. I know it was hard for thee to accept Father's words about John Shipling, but he was right in reminding thee of thy age. Thee is so young, and God has much in store for thy life."

"How old were thee and Father when thee were married?" I asked as I continued to mend the shirt in my lap.

"Well..." Mother began hesitantly, as though giving much thought as to what she might say. As I looked up, I thought I could detect a touch of pink rising in her cheeks. "Your Father was eighteen, and I was sixteen. We felt it was God's will, and we had the approval of the Richmond Meeting as well," she finally admitted. "It was not always easy, however," Mother continued. "I was so young, and not always a good wife to your Father those first few years. I have often wondered if God might have had some special work for me had I not chosen to marry so young, but I will never know," she finished, almost wistfully.

This was a vulnerable side of Mother I had never seen before, and I began to understand her reluctance to see me make what she considered a mistake. Because of this openness, I felt I could now share with her what I had decided to do after we finished mending.

"I appreciate thy words, Mother, but thee knows I will have to make my own choices when it comes to marriage. I will try to follow thy wishes if at all possible. I know Father forbade me to see John, but I feel I have to see him at least once more to explain Father's position. I am meeting him this morning near the south woods. I know Father will be angry if he finds out, but I am telling thee because although I don't wish to disobey, it is something I feel I must do. I hope thee will not tell Father of my plans," I said, waiting for her reply.

"Thee is placing me in a difficult position, Rebecca. Thee knows I am to respect Alfred as the head of our home. To keep something from him is to be dishonest. I will have to pray about the matter before giving my word. I do thank thee for

*Treasure Hunter*

telling me," she finished with a grateful smile.

I had no trouble finding a reason to go to the south woods. Jezebel needed to be grazed, even though the ground was nearly frozen solid and green grass was sparse.

I walked slowly toward our meeting place. Although I had nearly an hour until the appointed time, I did not know what I could ever say to John to help him understand Father's position. When we finally arrived, I tied Jezebel to a tree and walked to the creek. November had arrived with a cold snap, and I did not think I could stay too long before being thoroughly chilled. I did not even know if John would come, especially after Father's talk with him in Salem.

Nearly an hour passed and I was reluctant to admit what I knew to be true: John was not coming. Turning to get the cow, I noticed a brightly colored object in the distance. Could it possibly be John? Almost running, tripping over fallen branches and dead vines, I could see that it was indeed John. He was running, too, and when we finally met, he threw his arms tightly around me and spun me in circles until I was nearly dizzy!

"I was so afraid you wouldn't be here!" John began, nearly out of breath but clearly relieved. "Father has been ill, and he asked me to run an errand for him this morning. I rode our poor horse as fast as I could, but I wasn't sure I could reach you in time! Seeing you standing here was joy to my soul!"

The lump in my throat was growing, and I wasn't sure I could speak. When I finally felt in control of my emotions, I began to try and explain how Friends believed they could marry only other Friends, and in fact were not even to associate with members of another faith. To do so would mean being disowned by the Society of Friends. Because of this particular belief, Father would not even let me associate with a Mormon. I wanted to tell him how I disagreed with Father, how I thought he was being unfair. In respect to

*FOR THE LOVE OF A FRIEND*

Father, I kept silent, pleading with my eyes for John to understand my feelings.

"I still don't understand why your Father doesn't like me, Rebecca. What kind of faith forbids a person from even seeing one of another religion?!"

"Does thee really believe Joseph Smith found the golden plates and wrote the Book of Mormon?" I couldn't help but ask.

"Joseph Smith was a great prophet! He was as great as John the Baptist, or the disciple John, or Peter. In some ways he was even as great as Christ!" John spoke emphatically, clearly believing his words.

All hope of convincing John to become a Friend began to die. If he felt that strongly about Joseph Smith, there was little hope he would renounce the Mormon faith.

"I must go, John. It will be past our dinner time when I reach home as it is. I am sorry thee can not call in our home. I would have liked that," I said regretfully.

"That doesn't mean we can't still see each other!" There was a pleading tone to John's voice. "Couldn't we meet here again? No one knew you were meeting me today, so we could do it again. Would you meet me in two weeks?"

"I can't give thee my word, John, but I will think seriously about thy request. Thee knows it would be against Father's wishes, and I don't want to displease him."

"When will you be old enough to make your own decisions?" John asked angrily.

"I will try," was my final word as I turned to leave.

"Please come! Let's plan on two in the afternoon so we will have more time," John called as I started toward home.

The walk back went much too quickly, and my heart was in turmoil. I cared so much for John, much more than I was willing to admit to anyone, and I wanted to do as he asked. I also knew that as a child of God, I was expected to obey my parents. Was it possible John was correct in feeling I was old enough to make my own decisions? Would I be able to make

70

*Treasure Hunter*

the right choices?

Just as the cabin came in sight, I noticed a strange gray horse tied to the cow shed. Who could be visiting us on a Friday? As I came closer, a figure appeared in the cabin door that I quickly recognized: Betty!

Nearly running the legs off Jezebel, I ran as fast as she would allow! Quickly shutting her in the shed, I ran to greet my friend.

Grabbing her in much the same way John had grabbed me earlier, I hugged her until she laughed!

"Rebecca! I am glad to see thee, too!" she teased.

"I have so much to tell thee, Betty! Can thee stay a while?" I finally asked.

"I have much to tell thee as well, Rebecca! And yes, I can stay for a bit, just as long as I am home before dark."

Then I remembered! Betty's idea! She was here to tell me her plan! There was, after all, a light at the end of this very dark day!

# Chapter 10

# Promise Fulfilled

"Betty, I am so glad to see thee! I can't begin to tell thee how glad I am!" I repeated happily as Betty and I walked toward the cabin. "I had almost forgotten thy promised visit...we made a trip to Salem on Tuesday, and since then I...well, I have had a lot on my heart and mind," I explained.

"I'm sorry I couldn't get here any sooner," Betty apologized. "I knew thee would be anxious to hear of my plan, but it took longer than I expected."

"No, my restlessness was not due to thee..." I wanted to share with Betty my terrible dilema regarding John, but I was not sure how she would feel about me if she knew I were interested in a Mormon. I could not risk losing her friendship. "It was a family problem," I finally said, lamely.

"I trust it was nothing too serious?" she asked anxiously.

"It was and is a serious matter, but it is something I must deal with personally. I can't wait to hear your plan," I said enthusiastically, hoping to steer her thinking away from my problem.

"I'm so excited, Rebecca, and I hope thee will be as well!"

As we reached the cabin, Mother and Abigail were heading toward the cow shed to help Father and Jacob, although I was not sure any extra help was needed. I had a feeling Mother knew how important it was for Betty and me to have a little time to ourselves.

73

FOR THE LOVE OF A FRIEND

"Would thee care for a cool drink of water?" I asked as we sat down at the table.

"It is kind of thee to ask, Rebecca, but I must return soon and I want to have every minute possible to discuss my idea."

"If thee doesn't tell me this very minute, I shall die from curiosity!" I exclaimed.

Taking my hands in hers, Betty began to tell me of the wonderful plan that would change my life. "How would thee like to be a teacher?"

"That is the same question thee asked me on the Sabbath. As I told thee then, I believe I would like to teach, but I cannot be certain. Does thee know of another school in need of a teacher?"

"No," Betty said slowly, "but there is a school that does need thee—EAST GROVE SCHOOL! Does thee remember Father saying there would be a possibility of twenty children from Friends' families in this area?"

"Yes, but thee can teach..." I started to answer, still not understanding.

"No, I do not think I can manage to teach twenty children from the ages of five to fourteen without some assistance. I have never taught a single student before now, Rebecca! Thee has at least taught thy brothers and sister at home!"

"I have never heard of one school with two teachers, Betty. How would it be possible for both of us to teach?"

"Does thee think we could work together?" Betty asked, looking at me expectantly.

"Yes, I believe we could, but there is so much I do not know..."

"If I were to be the head teacher, would thee be willing to be my assistant and work with the younger children? Thee would be teaching them to read and do simple sums. That would not be too difficult, would it?"

"I have already been working with Levi on simple words and sums," I began, excitedly as pictures of the future began to form in my mind. "I imagine teaching other children would

74

be quite similar!"

"Would thee be willing to have me prepare the lessons for all the children in order to have a regular progression of learning?"

"Yes, in fact, I would be happy for thee to lay out the order of learning," I replied.

"There is one other item thee should consider before saying 'yes'," Betty cautioned.

"What is it? It sounds like a perfect plan! I had no idea thee felt I would make a suitable teacher! I feel very honored thee asked me!"

Betty began rather slowly, as if uncertain whether or not I would approve of this one consideration. "The reason it required several days for me to present my idea to you, Rebecca, is because it was necessary for Father to speak to each of the elders of meeting, as well as each family with children attending classes to get their approval."

"Was there a problem?" I interrupted, my spirits beginning to sag a bit.

"There is no problem with your teaching ability," Betty added quickly, "but there is a problem with the wages."

"What is the problem?" I ask, nearly afraid of the answer.

"The elders did not feel they could ask families to support two teachers. They did not object, however, when Father told them I was willing to share my wages with thee. It would not be much, often only food for thy table," Betty hurried on nervously, "but it would help thy family in a small way."

Betty appeared to be holding her breath for my answer. As if I thought wages were that important!

"I would teach for no wages at all, Betty!" I exclaimed, relieved. "I am just so happy thee asked me to help teach! Thee knows how much learning means to me! Of course, I will have to ask permission from Father and Mother, but I know the high importance they place on a good education!"

"It will be a great deal of work, of course, planning and helping the children learn, but it will certainly be easier with

*FOR THE LOVE OF A FRIEND*

two than one!" was Betty's happy reply.

"I will go and ask permission now, then we can make our plans," I said, rising to leave.

"Rebecca," Betty said hastily, grabbing my hand, "I hope some day thee will feel thee can share thy "family problems" with me. I am a good listener, and I hope a good friend."

I quickly gave Betty a hug, tears stinging my eyes. I longed to spill the secret of my heart, but I wasn't quite yet ready. "I thank thee...more than thee can know. Let's go find Father and Mother and tell them the good news!"


As I had thought, Father and Mother both approved of my opportunity to help with the school. School was to commence one week from Monday, so Betty and I made plans to work at the school on Thursday and Friday in preparation. Mother and I spent several hours pouring over the few books we had brought from Richmond, sorting them into subject and ability level. My favorite book was one given me by Grandmother Burgess. It was an old book of maps, and I remembered looking up IOWA when we were planning our move, only to find it was not even a territory at the time the book was published! I still loved looking at the strange lands I would never visit, wondering how the people lived, what the land was like, and what kind of strange animals lived there. The more I looked through our books, the more excited I became. Would we be prepared for the first day of school less than one week away?

Father purchased a second horse from the Mendenhalls for me to ride to school with the last of his savings. I was grateful for his generosity, and I knew my days would be much easier if I did not have to walk the two miles to the school.

As I approached the school house on Thursday, I noticed Betty's horse already tied to a newly constructed hitching post. I knew I would have to arise early if I were to beat Betty to school! I quickly unloaded what supplies I had been able

*Promise Fulfilled*

to bring with me on the horse, and entered the cabin.

My heart sank as I looked around the four walls. The abandoned cabin was filled with a dampness from sitting empty for so long that quickly chilled my body as well as my soul. How would twenty children squeeze into this small cabin? How would they work with no desks?

Seeing my disheartened look, Betty smiled and said gently, "I know it doesn't look like a school yet, but it will, I promise! Someone is bringing wood for a fire, and many Friends will be here tomorrow to build the tables and benches. Come see the books Friends have loaned us already!"

Betty lead me to a crate in the corner where a number of books had been neatly stacked. There was nothing like a good book to cheer me up, and the sight of so many immediately worked wonders. I was known as the book worm in our family, a title I did not deny nor dislike. In many ways I felt books might be my only glimpse of life beyond East Grove. Looking at the many volumes gathered, I began to feel a growing excitement as I thought of teaching the children on Monday.

Betty and I sorted through the books and began to make plans for our respective duties. Betty had a list of students, and there were eight children who would be in my care. When she asked if I would consider using the loft for my instruction, I quickly agreed. By having an area of my own, I would really feel like a teacher, not just someone's helper. Carefully climbing the ladder to the loft, I was soon mentally picturing where my students and I would sit learning. When the cabin door burst open sending a blast of cold air up the ladder, I was quickly brought back to reality. That must be the person Betty said was bringing wood, I thought to myself gladly, as I heard the logs hit the stone fireplace. A fire would feel good right now as my fingers and toes were chilled to the bone inspite of my thick woolen socks and gloves. Climbing down the rungs of the ladder, I felt two hands fit snugly around my waist to support me-as if I were going to fall! "Betty, thee must think

*FOR THE LOVE OF A FRIEND*

I'm pretty helpless!" I laughed, turning to tease her.

"Wha..." I sputtered, "What do you think you're doing?!!"

"Why, I was just helping thee down the ladder," Joshua said with that annoying grin of his. "Thee would not want to fall and hurt thyself so close to the beginning of school!"

Trying to contain my burning anger, I turned to Betty, choosing to ignore this unwelcome intruder. "Does thee need any further assistance today? If not, I shall return home to further plan my lessons," I said stiffly.

"I'm sorry, Rebecca," came Joshua's surprising words. "I didn't mean thee any harm," he finished with a slight smile.

Still choosing to ignore him, although caught off guard by his apology, I looked expectantly at Betty for her answer.

"I think we have done all we can do for today, Rebecca. When the men finish with the benches tomorrow, we will set the books out in preparation for Monday." Turning to Joshua, she added warmly, "Thank thee for bringing the firewood, Joshua. It will be so helpful to have a fire built each day this winter to warm us." Looking my way, she continued a bit uneasily, "Oh, by the way Rebecca—did I tell thee Joshua has promised to prepare a fire for us each day so the cabin will be warm when we arrive? We are lucky he lives so close to the school! It will be wonderful to start on our lesson plans as soon as we arrive each day."

"That is nice of thee, Joshua," I said without enthusiasm. Being polite to Joshua was going to take some practice, but I had decided after Betty's earlier chiding for my treatment of him, that perhaps she was right—he was a child of God and I tended to treat Jezebel better than Joshua!

Turning to leave, Joshua looked back at Betty with a smile. "I hope the school goes very well for thee, Betty. Thee will be good with the children."

I thought Betty looked a bit flushed as she looked away shyly. "Thank thee, Joshua. I appreciate thy kind words."

Joshua left abruptly, not even looking my way. Turning toward Betty, a strange feeling began to emerge within me,

*Promise Fulfilled*

one I was not comfortable with. Why should it bother me if Joshua gave Betty a compliment? Maybe they would even be married someday...I didn't think Betty would object to that idea. So why did it seem to be bothering me?

Vowing to think of nothing but school, I bid farewell to Betty and headed for home. The November air was cold, but I let the horse walk slowly toward our cabin. I felt my life was about to be changed in some significant way, but I had no control over that change. A ship at sea in a storm, that's what my life was, I decided. At least I still had a week before making a decision about seeing John again, for which I was grateful. I was afraid that the week was going to pass too quickly for comfort, but at least maybe I would be at peace once I had made my choice.

## Chapter 11

# Choices

School began on schedule and the children arrived in a state of great excitement. I hoped they would be as excited on the last day as they were today! My task would be especially difficult, for if children began to dislike learning at an early age, it would be very difficult to help them as they grew older. Jacob was a prime example of that very problem! He had not wanted to crawl out from under the quilts this morning, which was not like him at all. In fact, Jacob was usually the first child to rise, and he often milked Jezebel before breakfast. This morning, however, Father had to call him three times before his feet hit the cold wooden planks of the loft! His dislike of school had begun when he was only six years old. Our teacher had been a stern task master—short on praise, long on criticism. Jacob had been afraid to recite for fear of making a mistake, and by the end of the school session, he was vowing to quit school. I hoped Betty would be able to ignite the spark of interest in learning that I knew was within Jacob, however deeply it might be buried. He was such a good child, though stubborn at times, and I hated to see him dislike something as important as his education.

We settled quickly into what would become our daily school routine: Scripture reading and prayer, a brief time of singing, and our lessons. When the opening exercises were finished, I took my eight small, but eager, pupils to the loft to begin their schooling. It seemed like we had just begun to

*FOR THE LOVE OF A FRIEND*

know each other when Betty called for us to join her group in a short time of play outside. It did not take long for the children to lose their shyness with each other and begin a vigorous game of Red Rover.

"How does thee like teaching?" Betty asked eagerly once the children were playing well on their own. "It is wonderful—so far!" I laughed. "I have only been teaching for two hours, but I really believe I am going to enjoy it! Did everything go as expected with thy students?"

"They are going to be a wonderful group, Rebecca, I am certain! There will be several challenging students, however. Since I will need the children to respect me, I will have to be extra firm with them now. Hopefully, once I gain their respect, we can relax a bit and enjoy what each of us has to offer."

"How is Jacob doing?" I was almost afraid to ask, but I had to know.

"I can not really tell thee. He has not said a word, spending most of his time staring out the window. Tomorrow I shall try seating him away from the window...of course, he will probably then gaze at the floor!" Betty laughed. "Seriously, though, I sense a pain within Jacob that hurts me as well. It is my fervent prayer that before this session is finished, we will have begun to sooth and heal the wound."

I gazed admiringly at Betty. She had spent two hours with my brother and already understood his agony. Would I ever be that sensitive?

"We had best get the children inside and finish our morning lessons," Betty announced after a few more minutes had passed. "Lunch time will be here before we are finished with this morning's work!"

And so our day went. Lessons, recess, lessons, lunch, lessons, recess, lessons, dismissal. How had the time passed so quickly? Betty and I wearily sat down together to assess our first day. We both agreed it had been challenging, but rewarding. The light in Jeremiah Hoskin's eyes as he had read

82

his first words would be something I would always carry in my heart. Yes, I was going to love teaching. Betty and I both felt a need to prepare more material for each day's lessons, and have shorter recesses! The children had had so much fun playing it had been difficult for them to settle down and refocus their thoughts toward learning!

Gazing at the dying coals in the fireplace, I realized Joshua must have been there very early to start the fire. I had to admit it was generous of him to come early each day, but I was still glad he had left this morning before I arrived.

"Are there any teaching aids thee needs from Salem, Rebecca?" Betty asked, rising to bank the fire. "Father will ride to Salem tomorrow to pick up the supplies we need for the school. I have made a list for him, but I would be glad to add anything thee might like."

"It would be nice to have some slates," I began slowly, not wanting to seem extravagant. "Only one of my students was able to bring one today. I know they are quite an expense," I added quickly, "so I will make do without them if thee needs more important things."

"I will add them to the list, and if there are not enough funds to purchase everything, Father will have to choose which things to buy. I'll finish straightening the furnishings here," Betty continued, "so thee can go on home."

Gathering my things, I prepared to leave. Jacob, Abigail, and Levi had left with the other children when school had been dismissed, but as they were walking, I was certain they had not yet reached home. If I hurried, we could take turns riding the horse, two at a time.

The trail home was not dangerous, though there was the creek to cross. It was nearly frozen, and soon we would be able to walk on the ice. For now, a large tree which Father had felled across the creek served as our "bridge". The children's imaginations had created many stories and fantasies centering around this magical crossing. As I approached the creek, I could see all three playing on the moss covered log, something

*FOR THE LOVE OF A FRIEND*

Father would not be pleased with! He had warned the children of the dangers of playing over the cold rushing water, as none of them could swim well in the swift current.

"Jacob! Thee is to be responsible for thy brother and sister!" I said sternly as I approached.

"I AM responsible, Rebecca! They are not LOST are they?!" he said with a mischievous grin.

"Thee knows what I mean!" I retorted, having a hard time sounding gruff. Jacob might not get high marks in school, but there was certainly nothing wrong with his mind!

"If thee will all hurry, we can take turns riding home on the horse," I said encouragingly.

"Rebecca, when is thee going to name thy horse?" Abigail said with a giggle. "Thee can't keep calling it "the horse" forever!"

"Thee is right, Abigail," I answered with a laugh, "but I just haven't been able to think of a suitable name. Do any of you have a good one?"

"How about Jonah?" Levi asked innocently. "This horse's belly is almost as big as a whale's, and that reminds me of Jonah!"

We all laughed at the thought of Jonah inside the horses's belly!

"I like the name Joshua," Abigail began, "because he went into the promised land and told the others to follow him and not be afraid. This horse is not afraid of anything, either!"

"I think one Joshua in the community is enough," I said with grim determination. Imagine the smug look on Joshua Frazier's face if he were to learn my horse was his namesake!

"Jacob, does thee have an idea?" I asked.

"What does thee think of Samson?" Jacob asked tentatively, unsure about sharing his idea. "He was the strongest man in the Bible, and this horse is stronger than any of us!"

"He was strong," Abigail interjected, "but not very smart! He told Delilah the secret of his long hair, and she cut it off. He lost his power and everyone laughed at him!"

84

*Choices*

"Yes," Jacob argued, "but he was wise in the end because he asked God to give him his strength back and he pulled the pillars of the temple down and killed all those people who had laughed at him!"

"I am going to be sure and tell Father how well thee have all been listening to his scripture readings each night!" I said, thinking about their proposed names. "Thee all have good suggestions, but I think I am going to choose Jacob's name: Samson. Just as Samson cried out for God's strength in defeating the enemies, Jacob is wise to realize it is never too late to learn new lessons," I finished, smiling gently at this rapidly maturing brother. I had a feeling Betty would soon be helping Jacob fulfill this lesson in his own life.

Taking turns riding, we soon reached our destination where Mother was waiting anxiously for news of our day. The children had difficulty taking turns describing the many new experiences they had enjoyed. Even Jacob spoke of the fun he had playing games at recess! Levi seemed especially proud to be the brother of his teacher, though I had tried my hardest to treat each pupil equally and show no favoritism. Levi was a quick learner, and I would soon have to think of new ways to challenge him.

"And how did thee enjoy thy first day?" Mother asked finally, turning to me.

"I really enjoyed it," I said honestly. "It is going to be hard work, but seeing the children learn is a wonderful experience!"

There was a warmth in Mother's eyes, as well as a hint of sadness. "I am so glad thee likes to work with the children, Rebecca. I always thought I might like to teach," she said wistfully, "but thee was born a year after our marriage, so there was no time to consider anything but motherhood." She was silent for a moment, as if reflecting on another time and life.

"Well, you all have your chores to do, so we had best get busy!" Mother finally said with a bright smile, brushing away a single tear as though casting aside what was in the past.

85

*FOR THE LOVE OF A FRIEND*

Abigail, Jacob and Levi went outside to tend to the livestock. We were now the proud owners of two brown setting hens, which were Abigail's responsibility. She delighted in finding the hens' warm eggs, but the pecking beaks would sometimes cause her temper to fly! Jacob was still responsible for milking Jezebel, and Levi helped Father feed the hogs. Helping Mother with supper was my daily chore. I could prepare any dish she could, and I often tried to think of new ways to spice up the familiar recipes. It was a time of closeness for the two of us, even though minutes were often short. Mother had not said a word about John Shipling since that Friday when I had told her of my intention to see him. I knew she had to be thinking about it, so it was no surprise when she finally mentioned the subject.

"I trust thee saw young John Shipling when thee went to the woods on Friday?" she began hesitantly.

"Yes." I was not certain how freely I should discuss the matter with Mother, as I knew she felt a certain obligation to keep no secrets from Father.

"Does thee plan to see him again?" she asked cautiously.

I was not expecting such a direct question. I was certain Father had discussed the matter with her already, so she was aware of his forbidding me to see John.

"I am not certain," I finally said, trying to be honest without revealing too much. I would have to hope Mother would keep my confidence.

"I have been praying for thee night and day since last week, Rebecca. I know thee will do what the Spirit leads."

"I thank thee for that, Mother." I said, truly grateful.

I sensed there would be no more discussion, for Mother had spoken what was on her heart. I wanted my life to be Spirit led, as she said, but I was having difficulty sensing just what that leading was. When I knelt each night, thoughts of John's warmth and kindness kept interrupting my prayers. Friday would be here, sooner than I wished, and my choice would have to be made. Could I be happy with teaching alone?

*Choices*

Could I risk saying no to what might be my only chance at a happy marriage? Marrying John would mean leaving the Society of Friends. Could I be happy in the Mormon faith, knowing what I did about Joseph Smith and the Book of Mormon? And what of the Mormon belief of polygomy? Could I handle John taking a second wife if he chose to do so?

As I buried my head under the quilt before falling asleep, I sensed my decision was more than I could manage alone. Speaking to God as I would a friend, I simply asked Him to help me make the right choice. I also asked Him for some sort of sign, like Gideon and the golden fleece. Hadn't Father just read in the book of James tonight, "If any of you lack wisdom, let him ask of God?" I was certainly in need of some wisdom, I thought sleepily, especially where John was concerned. God would have to provide it, for time was nearly gone, and the choice would soon have to be made.

**Chapter 12**

# A Letter From Heaven

Betty brought the new supplies her father had purchased in Salem to school on Tuesday. She seemed to be very excited about something, something more than just the thought of new slates and pencils!

"Betty, what secret is thee keeping from me?" I finally asked, the curious side of my nature getting the best of me.

"Well, is thee certain thee wants to know?" she asked mischievously, her eyes gleaming with some secret knowledge.

"Yes, thee knows I do. What has gotten thee so excited?" I questioned.

"This!" she exclaimed, pulling a long battered envelope from underneath a slate. "It is a letter from someone by the name of Burgess. Does thee know of anyone by that name?"

Burgess! It had to be from Grandmother Burgess, but where had it come from? Heaven?!

"Where did thee get this?" I asked wonderingly, looking excitedly at the envelope in my hands.

"When Father went to Salem yesterday, the owner of the General Store said he had a letter for someone in East Grove, and would Father take it. A new settler coming from Richmond had delivered it on his way through. Thee is so lucky to receive a letter, Rebecca!" Betty said with a clear note of jealousy in her voice, although I was sure she was happy for me.

89

*FOR THE LOVE OF A FRIEND*

"I can't believe Grandmother's letter got here so quickly! I had Father leave a letter at the General Store for Grandmother in September, but the owner said it might be months before someone was traveling east to deliver it! I never thought I would hear from her so fast!" I said incredulously, still staring at this small blessing.

"Is thee going to open it, or just stand in awe?" Betty asked teasingly.

Being careful so as to preserve the envelope, I gently extracted Grandmother's lengthy letter. Although the handwriting was a bit ragged, I savored every word of news related. Grandmother told of happenings at Richmond Friends Meeting, and the new millinery being built down the street from her home. She said Maude was doing well now, but she had sorely missed me for some time after our departure. Grandma Wilson was feeling well, and was so glad she had not tried to make the trip to Iowa. There was other news as well, but it was the last sentence of her letter that burned itself into my memory.

"Never forget thou art blessed of God, Rebecca, and destined to do great things When thee must make choices, follow thy head first and then thy heart as God speaks to our intellect, helping us make wise decisions."

A jolt of understanding coursed through my soul as I suddenly knew what my choice would be regarding John. If I had been listening to my head instead of my heart, I could have saved myself many sleepless hours!

"What is it, Rebecca? Thee looks like the calm after a raging storm. That must have been a powerful letter!" Betty finally said as I continued to stare at the writing that jumped out of the page at me.

"Betty, does thee believe in miracles?" I asked, still dazed.

"Well," she said slowly, "I believe in the miracles re-

90

corded in God's Word."

"No, I mean modern day miracles."

"I suppose if God could perform miracles during Bible times, He can still perform them today. Why?" she asked, more puzzled than before.

"This letter is a miracle, Betty. It came on the exact day I needed it, and it contained the exact words I needed to hear! Remember the family problem I mentioned the day thee came to ask me about helping thee teach?"

"Yes..."

"This letter contains the answer to the problem! Thee has seen a miracle today, Betty!" I finished with a sense of awe.

"That is wonderful, Rebecca! I know the problem thee has been wrestling with has been a heavy burden. I have been praying for thee since the first day thee mentioned it to me!" Betty exclaimed. "I know God answers prayers, but this is the first time I have seen a prayer answered by a miracle!" she finished as she gave me a hug. "Now if we don't quit talking, the children will be here and we will have nothing for them to work on today!"

We quickly finished last minute preparations just as the children began to arrive one by one. The day passed quickly as did the rest of the week. When Friday arrived, I knew what I must do: I had to see John one last time and tell him my decision.

Finishing my work at school as quickly as possible, I said farewell to Betty and headed for Samson at the hitching post. If I took a short cut to the south woods, I could still see John and be home about the same time as always. Spurring Samson on, we covered the distance in record time. I did not know if John would still be waiting for me, as it was nearly two hours past our appointed time. My heart was pounding as I approached our meeting place in the south woods. Sure enough, I could see John in the distance working on the fence, his golden hair relecting the last rays of the setting sun.

"John! It's Rebecca! Can thee talk to me for a moment?"

*FOR THE LOVE OF A FRIEND*

I called after dismounting Samson.

"Rebecca!!" John shouted joyfully, dropping his axe and beginning to run toward me. This was not going to be easy, I thought, as the familiar handsome face came into view.

"Rebecca, Rebecca, Rebecca..." John kept repeating over and over as he held me tightly against him, as if he could not believe I was truly there in the flesh.

Breaking free from his grasp, I began what I knew was going to be the hardest thing I had ever done in all my fifteen and a half years. "John, I have made a decision with regard to seeing thee," I began nervously.

"Before you tell me your decision," John interrupted excitedly, "let me tell you my news. It might make a great difference in our lives!"

"All right, what is it?" I asked curiously, not minding putting off the unpleasant task of telling him my decision.

"I don't know how much you know about The Church of Jesus Christ Latter Day Saints, but you asked me before about Joseph Smith, so I assume you also know he was brutally murdered in Nauvoo this past June. Father felt the group would fail without a leader, thus his decision to remain in Iowa. We have just learned, however, that a brilliant man by the name of Brigham Young has agreed to assume leadership of our people. He has a vision of leading us to the promised land of Salt Lake City in Utah. Father has decided to join the others in Nauvoo to prepare for the journey."

So John was leaving East Grove, and I had spent all that time worrying for nothing. His next words, however, nearly took my breath away.

"I would like to ask you to marry me, Rebecca! I know your father does not approve of my religion, but we would be leaving Iowa to live in paradise! If you can't go with us now, we would stop for you when we pass through the area on our journey west!" John finished, looking imploringly at me.

It was one of those moments a girl dreams for, but it turns out to be the wrong thing at the wrong time. I had thought of

*A Letter From Heaven*

marrying John Shipling many times these past few months, yet I had no idea he, too, was thinking of marriage. Now he was proposing just that, and I was going to close the door.

"John," I began slowly, "I cannot marry thee."

"Why.."

"Please let me finish before I lose my courage!" I begged. "I have admired thee since the first day I met thee at the cabin raising. I knew our faiths were different, but I didn't believe it was important enough to keep us apart. Even when Father revealed some aspects of your religion I knew were contrary to the Holy Scriptures, I was still not willing to say no to your request to see me. I have prayed for God's wisdom to know His will for my life, and this week God showed me He is still performing miracles. Thy religion worships many gods, John, and God's Word says there can be only one God. Thy people consider Joseph Smith to be a saint, but he was only a treasure seeker and deceiver. We could never worship together, nor be in agreement on spiritual matters. The Society of Friends may not be perfect, but they have shown me the way to truth, and I will not abandon them," I said with a rush of breath, suddenly feeling completely drained.

Grabbing my hands in his, John began to plead. "Rebecca, I love you! Surely that could overcome any differences we might have where religion is concerned!"

Finally able to smile, knowing I had made the right choice, I looked fully at John. "Thee is a kind man, John Shipling, yet I hardly know thee nor thee me. I am sure thee will find a woman of thy own faith who will love thee and honor thee. I wish thee well, John," I said, gathering Samson's reins in my hand. "I must go now, or the others will wonder why I have not returned from school."

"All right, Rebecca, if you are certain. I also wish you well, but I believe your religion is too narrow-minded and unyielding. We could have had a wonderful life together!" John finished sadly, turning to leave. "If you are sure I cannot persuade you to come with me, I suppose this is good-bye."

*FOR THE LOVE OF A FRIEND*

"We Friends prefer to say 'farewell', John, rather than good-bye. No parting is final for true believers, for we know if we do not meet again on this earth, we will be reunited in heaven."

Managing a smile, John waved. "Very well, then, farewell, Rebecca. You are a special woman who will make some man very lucky one day!"

"I thank thee, John. Farewell to thee. I hope thee will find thy promised land!"

Climbing quickly upon Samson, I headed straight for the cabin. I knew the others would be watching for me, and I also knew I would have to give an answer for the direction of my return. But I was ready to be honest after the manner of Friends once more. I began to realize all the times I had stretched the truth where John was concerned. How could I have ever thought there might be a future with this man?

I felt freer and lighter than I had in months. A great peace spread through me as Samson galloped home, the brisk air whipping the loose strands of hair about my face. With God's leading through Grandmother Burgess, I knew I had made the right choice. Now I would have to trust God to prepare that special man for me when His timing was right. For the present, I would be content with my teaching assignment, my good friend Betty, and my family and friends at meeting. I had learned a great deal this week, and I felt good about my future, whatever the Spirit led me to do.

# Chapter 13

# Winter's Fury

I don't like the looks of those black clouds in the west," Father remarked anxiously as he returned from early morning chores. "Thee will need to watch the skies, Rebecca, and ride home if a blizzard seems imminent."

The January skies often appeared forboding, though they had seldom yielded more than a skiff of flakes, or gusty winds. Snow had fallen on several occasions, but the warm southern winds which occasionally blew our way soon melted the white fluff. As a family, we were prepared for the inevitable: a snowstorm of fierce proportions that could easily harm or even kill man or beast. Father had instructed each of us to remain in the cabin should any sign of a blizzard appear. Under no circumstances were we to try and travel-not even the short distance to the cow shed-while the wind and snow storm raged outside.

Our family felt as prepared for the terrible storms as we could possibly be, and we children were secretly anticipating the first blizzard's arrival. There was nothing quite as fun as walking over mountainous drifts of snow as tall as the cabin; nor anything quite as beautiful as the glittering landscape reflecting the sun's rays following the storm.

December had passed quite calmly with the meager snow- falls quickly melting.

Christmas had been observed in the simple manner of

*FOR THE LOVE OF A FRIEND*

Friends. The account of the saviour's birth had been shared and pondered, including the tale of the wise men and their gifts for the Christ child. We knew children from other beliefs would be receiving many gifts, some quite useless, but we were happy with the small tokens given us by our parents: a new axe for Jacob, a shiny knife for Levi, a hand-sewn doll for Abigail, and a beautiful, soft blue shawl for me. I knew Father had traded one of the hogs for the purchased items, and I felt a new awareness of the depth of his love for his children.

Mother had roasted one of the hens for our special noon communion together, making the day a memorable one for each of us.

School continued to progress satisfactorily. My students were now reading simple picture books and putting their own words together to write simple stories. I loved the excitement in their voices as they deciphered words to add to their vocabularies and the light of discovery in their eyes when they learned something new. Betty continued to sooth and heal the deep hurt in Jacob, and each day saw him bloomimg in new ways as she gently praised and encouraged him. I enjoyed working with Betty as I found she had a wonderfully creative mind which made learning fun and exciting for the children instead of a dull burden.

It was our newest learning idea which occupied my mind as I rode to school that day, anxiously looking to the west for signs of the snowstorm that had Father so concerned. I knew if he felt there was any danger, he would not let the others walk today, nor would many of the other families with children in our school.

Betty's horse was already outside the cabin when I arrived. Huge snowflakes were just beginning to fall, so we would have to be especially watchful as the morning progressed.

"How art thou?" came Betty's greeting as I pushed open the heavy cabin door.

"I am well, but it is beginning to snow," I informed her as

96

*Winter's Fury*

I took off my thick wraps.

"I wonder if we will have our first blizzard today? I hope none of the children start for school if the snow gets heavier," she said rather anxiously.

"It is nearly an hour before we take up school, so perhaps we will know before then if there is to be a storm and of what proportions it might be."

"At least we have a good supply of wood if the wind begins to howl. Joshua has been chopping and cutting our supply for so long we must have a mountain of wood behind the cabin!" Betty said with a laugh.

"I should think he could find better things to do than come here and chop wood every day!" I said judgmentally, still unable to compliment Joshua for his hard work. "His father must certainly need him for something!"

"I am very grateful to Joshua for taking care of our needs," Betty said defensively. "Would thee like to chop the wood and build the fire each day?"

"No, I suppose I wouldn't," I said grudgingly.

"I think I'll check outside before we get started with today's plans."

There was a look of concern on Betty's face when she returned. "The snow is getting heavier, and I'm sure the wind is beginning to blow harder. Does thee think we should close up the school and start for home?"

Deciding to see for myself just how bad it was, I headed out the door. Betty was right about the snow: it was much heavier than the first few flakes that had floated lazily from the sky when I had first arrived. The wind, however, did not seem to be blowing much at all.

"I don't think we have a blizzard yet, anyway," I reported reentering the cozy warmth of the cabin. "If there are children walking right now, what would they do if they arrived to find an empty cabin? I think we should stay here at least for a while after their usual time of arrival."

"I suppose thee is right, Rebecca. I would just hate to be

97

caught trying to get home in the storm," Betty agreed reluctantly.

We began to work on the day's lessons, although it was certainly difficult to keep our minds centered on the work. Betty continued to raise her head every few minutes to listen for the wind, and I was beginning to think she must be somewhat of a worrier. This was a side of Betty I had not observed before, as she was always the picture of control. I had seldom seen her upset or worried over anything!

"Rebecca, I'm going to check the sky again," Betty finally said after she had asked me to repeat my latest idea three times!

She returned in a rush. "Rebecca, come quickly!"

Dashing out the door, I was totally unprepared for the blast that hit me! Snow was blowing in thick howling sheets, blocking out even the nearest trees. The horses were stamping nervously, as if they knew something were about to happen, and they wanted no part of it!

Hurrying back to the security of the cabin, we had to consider what to do. I knew the storm would get much worse before it was over, so our decision must be made quickly. There would surely not be any children coming now with the storm in full force, unless there happened to be some who had started early. Just thinking of that possibility made me shudder. Thoughts of Jacob, Abigail, and Levi walking in this storm were terrifying. Surely Father would not have let them start for school in the blinding snow!

"Does thee think we should go back to our homes?" Betty asked , casting nervous glances toward the window.

"I suppose we could try," I said with little enthusiasm.

"Let's hurry and get our wraps on so we can get started," Betty burst out, rushing for her heavy coat. "Maybe we can ride together the long way so we have only a short distance to go separately."

Hurrying out the door into the raging fury of the full-blown blizzard, we made sure the cabin was secured before climbing on our mounts. Riding as closely as physically

*Winter's Fury*

possible, we set out for our homes. Father's words, 'never go out in a blizzard' were beginning to haunt me as we tried to see our now white path. The winds seemed to shriek his warning, taunting me as we struggled on. Sensing we were in danger, I quickly prayed for our safe arrival home.

The horses were now staggering, as if uncertain where to even take the next step. Betty looked like a white statue as the snow was driven into her clothing, and I was sure I looked the same. Sensing the foolishness of our efforts, I finally stopped Samson.

"What is it?" Betty shouted over the howl of the wind.

"I think we should go back before we are become totally lost!" I yelled back.

Nodding in agreement, we turned and started back for the schoolhouse. Hoping the horses would sense our helplessness, we rode as quickly as possible, trying to follow our now completely snow covered tracks. Keeping my head down to prevent the driving snow from stinging my wind burned face, I nearly tumbled head first into a snowdrift when Samson suddenly stopped with a jerk.

"What is it, Samson?" I asked angrily, my voice quickly lost in the shrieking wind. "Take us to the cabin! We can't waste precious time standing around in this blizzard!"

When Samson still refused to move, I reluctantly climbed down. It was then I stumbled upon the reason for Samson's actions. Lying on the ground was a mound of white, the form of a child!

"Betty!!" I screamed, horrified.

Sensing the urgency in my voice, she quickly dismounted.

"It's one of the children!" Gently we turned the still warm and faintly breathing body to look into the unconscious and nearly frozen face of Matthew Cook. He must have stumbled and fallen as he tried to run the last few yards to the cabin. I shuddered to think of what would have happened if we had not turned back.

"Let's try and get him on Samson," I said quickly, "and I'll

99

lead him to the cabin."

"What about his sister, Naomi?" Betty yelled in my ear.

Naomi was Matthew's six-year-old sister, one of my pupils. Looking around in the snow, I gently stamped my feet in search of another body. I hated wasting precious moments looking for something I didn't know was there, but neither could I in good conscious leave a child to die in a blizzard! Having looked over the area as well as possible under the circumstances, I finally gave up my search.

"I didn't find anything, did you?" I shouted.

"No," Betty answered, a tremor in her voice. "I guess we should get Matthew loaded and return to the school."

It was a struggle, as Matthew was a husky nine-year-old who remained unconscious, despite our efforts to awaken him. We were fortunate to be within a few hundred yards of the cabin, and grateful to have two good horses to help lead us to our destination.

Soon we were safely inside the cabin, both of us carrying Matthew's limp form. We pulled one of the benches near the fireplace and carefully laid the still body close to the warmth of the fire. Betty took off his now soaked coat and hat and began to rub his hands and cheeks. I quickly picked up our water pail and ventured back out long enough to gather some snow to melt for our water supply.

"If thee would please get one of the rags we use to clean the slates, I would try to wipe some of the snow off Matthew," Betty said, never taking her eyes off the chubby face she held tenderly. Betty will make a wonderful mother someday, I thought admiringly.

With rag in hand, Betty wiped the snow off Matthew's face, neck and hair, continuing to speak to his lifeless body.

"Matthew, we need thee to wake up. Thou art safe now, and there is no reason for thee to remain asleep. Thou art a strong boy, and Rebecca and I may need thee to help carry wood for the fire," she continued with no respons

"Rebecca, would thee please come and pray for Matthew?

*Winter's Fury*

Betty asked, her voice quivering just a bit.Feeling the need to be a source of strength, I took Matthew's cold hand and began to pray.

"Father, thou knowest Matthew is thy child, and that he loves Thee. Thou also knowest Betty and I are not doctors, and we have no idea what to do for his body. Would thou please touch and heal him just now?" I prayed as simply and honestly as I knew how, believing God would answer my request. This was the first time I had ever prayed aloud in the presence of another person, and I hoped the prayer was sufficient.

Looking up at me, there were tears in Betty's eyes. "That was wonderful, Rebecca. I know God will answer thy prayer!"

We continued to rub Matthew's still cold body, visiting a bit now that we had placed Matthew's recovery in God's hands. I decided the time had come to share my past trial with John Shipling, and how God had provided the answer through Grandmother Burgess's letter.

"I knew that letter had a powerful effect on thee!" Betty exclaimed, the last piece of the puzzle complete. "I am so glad thee felt thee could share this part of thy life with me. I am also glad thee did not take off and marry John and leave me with twenty students to teach!" she said with a laugh.

"I had not even thought of that!" I said. "I suppose I was so caught up in trying to make a decision regarding a husband that school was the farthest thing from my thoughts! Thee knows I would not deliberately leave thee short-handed!"

"Betty!" I almost jumped off the chair as a desparate thought entered my mind. "What about the horses? They will freeze in this storm and then what will we do? We can't stay in this cabin forever with only two lunches for three people!"

"I had completely forgotten about the horses! Oh, I hope they haven't perished in this storm!" Betty cried.

"I'll go and check on them," I said with more courage than I felt. I had no idea where they might be, as we had simply abandoned them in our haste to get Matthew inside.

Putting on my damp wraps once again, I carefully opened

*FOR THE LOVE OF A FRIEND*

the door. The snow had drifted along the hinged side, but I still could manage to squeeze through the opening. "Samson," I began to call. "Samson, where art thou?"

Listening intently, I thought I heard a nicker coming from the south side of the cabin. Creeping slowly along the wall, making sure to keep in contact with the snowy logs, I saw the horses as I rounded the corner. Both were being protected by the huge stack of wood Joshua had piled for future use. For once, I thought, Joshua finally did something useful! The snow drifting around the edge of the wood pile was forming a natural enclosure which would protect the horses nicely from the howling wind and snow.

Returning to the cabin, I relayed the news of the horses' safety to Betty.

"That's just like Joshua—always planning ahead and saving the day!" she said admiringly.

I tried to hold back the sarcastic reply on my lips, knowing we really were fortunate Joshua had cut and stacked the wood.

Just then Matthew began to moan a bit and move his lips as if trying to speak. "Matthew! Wake up! It's Miss Jessop, and you are at school."

Matthew continued to groan and make sounds. Finally they began to make sense. "Naomi...Naomi...where's Naomi?"

"Matthew," Betty began slowly, afraid of what his reply might be, "was Naomi with you when you headed for school this morning?"

"Naomi...Naomi..." he continued to moan over and over again.

Looking at me, Betty put to words to the heavy thoughts on both our hearts. "Rebecca, do you think Naomi was with Matthew in the blizzard?"

"I don't know, Betty, but if she were, there is probably no chance she could survive the storm. If we tried to look for her, we would surely perish as well," I said gloomily. "We will have to hope someone was searching for her and found her," I finished, not really believing what I had just said.

102

*Winter's Fury*

As Matthew opened his eyes, he began to recognize his surroundings and started to get up.

"Just lie still," Betty commanded. "Thee has been unconscious for some time, and thee needs to rest."

"Is Naomi here too?" Matthew asked anxiously, looking around.

"Was she with thee in the storm?" I asked, not wanting to answer his inquiry just yet.

"Yes, we were walking to school early because Father wanted us to be sure and get here before the storm. Naomi got scared when it began snowing and started running back toward our cabin. I yelled and yelled at her to stay with me, but she wouldn't listen! I kept walking to school, but when it started to snow really hard, I couldn't find the path!" he finished as he began to sob.

"It will be all right, Matthew," Betty soothed. "I am sure Naomi is safe at home with your parents, and we will help thee get home as soon as the storm is over," she finished with more confidence than I was sure she felt.

Matthew eventually calmed down and drifted off to much needed sleep. As I carried more wood for the fire, I noticed an angelic smile had replaced the worry on Matthew's face.

"What does thee think has happened to Naomi?" Betty asked anxiously in a hushed voice.

"I'm sure she is safe at home, as thee told Matthew," I replied quietly. "But perhaps we should pray once more for her safety, as well as thank God for Matthew's recovery."

We each prayed silently this time, fervently asking God's watchful keeping over his precious child, while thanking him with all our hearts for Matthew's apparent healing.

When Matthew awoke again, we allowed him to sit up. We shared Betty's lunch of bread, cheese, and an apple, this being the first time we had eaten all day. Dark was fast approaching, and with the howl of the wind we realized we would be spending the night in the small schoolhouse.

Knowing it was important to keep Matthew's mind off his

103

*FOR THE LOVE OF A FRIEND*

sister, we played word games we knew he enjoyed in school, and then sang songs until our voices were nearly gone.

Pulling two more benches near the fire, we prepared for what we knew was going to be a long night. I made another trip to the wood pile to check on the horses and restock our supply. The tall drift across the door told me there would be no more trips out of the cabin until someone came to dig us out. I wondered if Father and Mother were worried about me, as well Betty's parents. Betty's mother had been ill the past several weeks, and I knew this was a great concern to her.

When we had settled in for the night, at least as well as possible on the hard wooden benches, Betty read from the book of Philippians, chapter 4 verse 19. "But my God shall supply all your need according to his riches in glory by Christ Jesus." It was the same verse Grandma Wilson had quoted to me before we left Richmond. It was a comfort to each of us to know that God would take care of all our needs here in this cabin in the middle of a raging blizzard. We would simply have to trust Him to send someone to help us when the storm subsided.

"I am so glad thee is here with me," Betty murmured drowsily as she drifted off to sleep.

"I am glad for thee, also," I replied, more to myself than Betty who was now fast asleep. The wind continued to drive the snow against the walls of the cabin, but I sensed God's loving arms surrounding us, and I felt at peace as sleep slowly overtook my weary body.

## Chapter 14

# Rescue the Perishing

When we arose early the next morning the wind was still, indicating an end to the previous day's blizzard. Peering out the small window of the cabin was pointless, as a huge snowdrift had blown from the peak of the roof across the clearing, effectively blocking any view of the outside world. I tried peeking though the door, but the drift which had been forming all during the previous day had effectively sealed us in the cabin.

"How art thou?" I greeted Betty in a whisper as she yawned, trying to awaken. Matthew was still sleeping like a baby.

"I had a less than comfortable night, but I am grateful we had the extra wood for warmth. Did thee put logs on the fire often?" Betty asked, looking at the now blazing fireplace.

"I am a light sleeper," I replied, "especially on a hard wooden bench! I put more wood on twice during the night, and again this morning. I felt it was important to keep the cabin as warm as possible for Matthew's sake."

We both looked at the calmly sleeping boy, aware that we had seen God's healing hand work a miracle in young Matthew's body. We still knew little of what had caused the unconscious state in which we had found him, but we assumed he had fallen and hit his head on the hard frozen ground.

"Miss Wilson, does thee think we will be found today?"

Matthew asked sleepily.

"Good morning, Matthew! Thee is looking well today!" I replied brightly. "I am not certain when we will be rescued, but I am sure our families are all worried about us and will start for the school as soon as possible."

"Would thee like some breakfast?" Betty asked a now fully awake Matthew.

"I sure would!" he exclaimed, rubbing his growling stomach.

It was my turn to share the lunch I had brought from home before the storm. We still had a bit of water in the pail which we used sparingly, not knowing when our next chance for more would occur.

When our meager breakfast was finished, Betty and I decided we would conduct school as if all twenty students were there. Matthew loved the idea, and he greatly enjoyed being the only pupil present! Neither Betty nor I could keep our minds on reciting, subtraction problems or geography lessons, however. Our ears were constantly on the alert for any sounds of our rescue.

Noon passed and we ignored the growls in our empty stomachs. Afternoon lessons were much the same as morning, with Betty and I growing more anxious with each passing minute. Would we have to spend yet another night here in this small snow-bound cabin? An even more disturbing thought was the fact that our wood supply was growing dangerously low. With no fire, we would surely freeze to death in a matter of hours! Not wanting to worry the others, I tried to be as cheerful as possible, as did Betty.

"I think school will be dismissed for the day," Betty said finally as we had covered nearly two days lessons already. Matthew would be ahead of the others his age now, so there was no point in advancing him further.

"Rebecca...did thee hear something?" Betty whispered excitedly in my ear. Straining to hear any noise at all, we could faintly detect scraping sounds outside the cabin. Jump-

*Rescue the Perishing*

ing up, we all ran to the door and began pounding on it.

"Help!! Help!! Matthew shouted. Betty and looked at each other in surprise. Matthew had been such a model prisoner we had no idea he was so worried about our predicament!

Unbolting the door and pushing the leather thong through the hole to the outside so it could be opened if someone were to pull on it, we stood back and waited anxiously. Our spirits were rising with each ping of the shovel. At last the door began to move, ever so slowly, and we knew our freedom was iminent. The figure at the door was nearly covered with the cold white snow, but it did not take long to recognize our rescuer.

Grabbing us together in a huge embrace, Joshua's voice gave away his true feelings.

"I am so glad you are safe! I am so glad you are safe!!" he kept repeating over and over.

I was not sure if he were speaking to any of us in particular, but it felt good to hear the words.

"Oh Joshua!" Betty was the first to respond. "I am so thankful to see thee! We were afraid we would have to spend another night here at school with no water, food, or fire wood! Thee is so brave to have risked thy life to come and save us!" I thought Betty was exaggerating just a bit. I was glad to be rescued, but surely someone would have gotten to the cabin eventually had Joshua not come—like Father, or Betty's father. Finally Joshua spoke.

"I'm afraid you will not be able to go home tonight as it is nearly dark and to try and travel in the snow without light would be too risky. If we hurry, however, we can reach my cabin where you can rest and partake of our supper with us. Has thee had anything at all to eat today?" he asked, looking at me worridly.

"Actually, we have done quite well for ourselves, Joshua," I replied, just a bit irritated. "If thee had not come, we were prepared to spend the night just as we did the last."

*FOR THE LOVE OF A FRIEND*

Looking at the one stick of wood lying near the hearth, that annoying grin spread across Joshua's face.

"What was thee going to do for wood, Rebecca? Burn the benches?!"

"If we had to," I said stiffly.

"We would never have survived, Rebecca, and thee knows it!" Betty said rather sharply.

"It does not matter now," Joshua broke in, "what matters is getting home before dark. Get your wraps and we can start out. Matthew can ride on my horse, and we adults can walk the short distance to our cabin."

Adults! That was a good one. Joshua was about as far from being an adult as Jacob was! Knowing the need for expediency, however, I chose to ignore the remark.

"Our horses! Joshua, did thee find our horses?" Betty asked anxiously, suddenly remembering our poor animals.

"No," Joshua said slowly, "I did not see any horses. Where might they be?"

Fearing the worst, we told him how the wood pile and snowdrift had made a natural shelter for them. Once again Betty sang Joshua's praises so loudly it nearly hurt my ears!

"Thee was so wise to chop and pile the extra wood, Joshua. I dread to think of the fate of our horses without thy hard work!"

"Well, let's just hope it was enough to keep them alive," Joshua said calmly.

Heading around the cabin, Joshua's voice could soon be heard. "They are all right!" he shouted, almost as though he couldn't believe his eyes. Soon he reappeared, leading the two horses behind him. I was so relieved to see Samson, I ran and hugged his neck. He had lived up to his name, and his strength helped him weather the storm.

Soon we were on our way, Matthew and Joshua doubled on Joshua's horse, with Betty and I following behind on our own mounts. As Joshua lived less than a quarter of a mile from the school, we were soon safe in his warm comfortable home.

108

*Rescue the Perishing*

Recounting our story once more for his family, we all rejoiced at our safekeeping, and the miracle of Matthew's rescue.

Following a hearty supper to fill our empty stomachs, Joshua's Father began the evening scripture reading to replenish our souls. As he closed his Bible, he looked pensive as if trying to organize his thoughts. At last he spoke quietly of the matter he had been considering.

"All of thee know Friends do not partake of the outward sacraments, particularly water baptism and communion, common to most religions. Although a sacrament represents something sacred, George Fox felt that when taken as a ritual or habit, it becomes meaningless. Since a sacrament is a visual expression of God's grace, all of life becomes a sacrament as we are constantly being reminded of the grace of God in our lives.

"The safe-keeping of you three young people during this storm is a wonderful expression of God's grace. As we have communion with God, let us be mindful of His grace and power in our lives!"

Our time of silent communion was one of the most meaningful I could remember. I had been the recipient of God's grace in my life before, but never in such a special way as in the last two days. When Joshua's father finally rose to replinish to the fire, I noticed Joshua staring at me. Perhaps it was the tears of joy that had trickled down my cheeks as I communed with God, or maybe it was something else, something known only to God and Joshua. Whatever the cause, I quickly looked away, not wanting to spoil the good feeling warming my soul. Joshua was going to be Joshua, and I would just have to learn to ignore him—if that were possible.

When Joshua's mother noticed Betty nearly fall from her chair, she insisted Betty and I spend the night in their bed.

"Father and I will sleep on the floor in front of the fire. Matthew can sleep in the loft with Joshua, and you young ladies will have the bed. Anyone who has survived a blizzard

*FOR THE LOVE OF A FRIEND*

by sleeping on a hard bench deserves a good night's rest!" she said firmly.

I was not going to argue, as my drooping eyes were trying to close in spite of my willing them open, and waves of drowsiness washed over my weary body.

As I lay in the unfamiliar but comfortable bed, I couldn't help but think of my family. I was sure they were terribly worried about Betty and me, and I prayed God would ease their minds in some way. Tomorrow we would be home again, and this would all be a memory we would store to tell our children. I was also worried about Naomi and her parents. What must they be going through? Even if Naomi had made it back to the cabin, they might have been searching all day in vain for Matthew. Adding them to my prayers was the last conscious thing I was able to do before sleep claimed me.


Joshua voluteered to escort Betty and me home the next day. His father would see that Matthew reached his own cabin safely.

"I believe I can make it home on my own," I began, not the least bit anxious to have Joshua take me home and receive a hero's welcome.

"I don't believe that would be wise, Rebecca," Mr. Frazier began, "the drifts are extremely deep and travel is difficult at best. Joshua has already been navigating the deep snow since the storm passed, so it will be in your best interest for him to accompany you to your cabin. He can ride with Betty first, since she is closer, then return for you."

Sensing the finality in his voice, I knew I would not be going home alone. I spent the morning helping Joshua's mother prepare the noon meal for the family. She was a pleasant woman, and we chatted amiably about school and meeting, ...and Joshua. Her concerns for her son were a surprise.

"I worry about Joshua. He is a wonderful son, but

110

*Rescue the Perishing*

sometimes he is so blind! I have seen the way Betty looks at him when they are together, but he seems to ignore her. She would make a wonderful helpmate for him, but I suppose I will just have to let him discover her interest on his own," she finished with a sigh.

Why should her words surprise me? I, too, had seen the adoring look in Betty's eyes whenever they were together. Not understanding how anyone could possibly find Joshua interesting, I had simply thought Betty was being her usual nice self where he was concerned. Why should I care if Betty was interested in that boy? Vowing to dismiss all thoughts of Joshua from my mind, I continued to think about returning home and seeing my family.

The trip home, however, was postponed until after the noon meal. This irritated me, because I didn't understand why we couldn't go before dinner. Joshua, however, insisted we eat the meal his mother had prepared before leaving.

Once we were finally on our way, I made no effort to carry on a conversation with my chauffeur. The way was treacherous, and often Samson would stumble, requiring all my concentration just to stay on his back. Joshua was uncharacteristically silent as well, which was fine with me. All I wanted was get home to my family!

Soon the familiar cabin was in sight, and Father came running out to meet us— moving as fast as the snow would allow!

Helping me off Samson, Father's unexpected embrace was strong and comforting.

"We have been trusting God for thy return," he began, "but we were concerned, nevertheless. It took all of yesterday for us to get out of our cabin, and when I was finally able to free us and ride to the school this morning, I could see by the shoveled snow that thee had already left. Not knowing where thee might have gone, I thought it best to return and pray for thy safe arrival."

Turning to Joshua, he added, "I thank thee for seeing

*FOR THE LOVE OF A FRIEND*

Rebecca safely home. Am I to assume thee is the one who helped them out of the school?"

"Yes, there was a sizable drift blocking the door, and they would have soon burned their entire supply of wood, not to mention their lack of food and water. I was happy to get them out when I did!" Joshua said thankfully.

Father shook Joshua's hand, grateful for all he had done. "Rebecca," he said turning to me, "does thee not wish to thank Joshua for his bravery in coming to thy rescue?"

Knowing I owed him at least that much, I said lowly, "Betty and I will always remember thy kindness, Joshua."

"Thee is welcome," Joshua said with his now familiar grin. "I had best be heading for home before darkness overtakes me. Farewell, Alfred." Then turning to me, "Farewell, Rebecca. I would be glad to save thee any time!" he finished before riding off.

Shaking off his last remark, I headed for the cabin and the rest of the family. After many hugs and tears came the recounting of the snowbound experience. Levi was especially glad to see me, never leaving my side until time for bed. I couldn't help giving him a special hug and whispering, "I love you."

I had not fully appreciated the closeness of our family until that night. Even after retiring to the loft, Abigail and I continued to whisper about the adventure.

"I wish I had been there with you," she sighed enviously. "Father refused to let us start for school when the snow began to fall. It would have been fun having school all by ourselves!"

"Matthew was there," I reminded her. And I still did not know about Naomi. Father thought we would have received the news by now if she had been lost in the storm, so I would just have to hope and pray she had made it back to her own cabin.

"I think I will be a teacher when I grow up," Abigail said sleepily. "Thee has all the fun!"

I smiled to myself. I would not call what I had just

*Rescue the Perishing*

experienced "fun", but teaching certainly was rewarding. Perhaps I would be a teacher all my life and never marry. That was certainly not unheard of. However I did not think it would be my choice!

## Chapter 15

# New Beginnings

The January blizzard proved to be the only major storm of the winter. Father had been correct in believing Naomi had made it safely back to her cabin the night we were snowbound with Matthew. There had been much rejoicing in the Cook family when they realized how close they had come to losing both their children.

As February passed into March, and March into April, the anticipation of spring was everywhere. The school children couldn't keep their minds on the daily lessons, all thoughts being centered on the recess of school. Father was spending more and more time working with the field equipment, preparing it for the planting season. Mother was planning a gigantic garden, realizing how important fresh produce was to settlers during the winter months.

East Grove Friends Meeting continued to grow, as did several of the others in our area. I had hoped a Quarterly Meeting would be organized soon with other Friends meetings in the area, but Father believed it would be quite some time before that would come to pass. We were in communication with some of the other churches in the area, and it was not uncommon for visitors to be present at meeting on any given Sabbath.

It did not surprise me, then, when Betty mentioned her family was preparing for visiting Friends from the Pleasant

*FOR THE LOVE OF A FRIEND*

Plain Meeting. They would be arriving sometime Saturday and staying overnight to join us for meeting on the Sabbath.

"Does thee know this family?" I asked her curiously.

"We have only met them one other time when they were traveling to Salem and somehow got on the wrong road. When Father learned they were Friends, he invited them to return sometime in the near future to visit East Grove Meeting," Betty explained, with an air of excitement.

"It would be nice to visit with a family from another meeting," I said wistfully. "I love my family, but we get a bit tired of each other's company at times!" "Will thy family be visiting on Saturday?" Betty asked. "Uh...well...I guess I didn't know we were invited!" I finally managed, not really understanding what she meant.

"Oh yes, Father gave an open invitation after meeting last week. Didn't thee hear him ask anyone with an interest in the Pleasant Plain Meeting to visit on Saturday?"

"I had almost forgotten!" I exclaimed, suddenly remembering why I hadn't known about the invitation. "We were not at meeting last Sunday because Father was not feeling well and Mother did not want to leave him alone. Father felt it best not to expose other members to our unknown malady."

"Then thee must be sure to tell thy father of our Saturday plans!" Betty exclaimed. "By the way," she added with a sly look, "their son is seventeen, and I think thee might like him!"

"Betty, I have decided to leave my future in God's hands. After my near disastrous experience with John Shipling, I am no longer seeking a husband!" I said with more conviction than I felt.

It had taken me all these months to put John out of my mind. I had to admit there were days when I still thought of him, wondering if he and his father were still in Nauvoo, wondering if Brigham Young had begun his journey to Salt Lake City, and the most painful question of all: had John found another woman to share his life with him?

Betty's words brought me back from the bittersweet past

116

*New Beginnings*

to the present. "Well, whether thee is interested in Luke or not, thee can still come and fellowship with us! Will thee ask thy father about coming?"

I wasn't sure why Betty was so insistent about our visit, but her excitement was contagious. "I really hope we will be able to come, Betty! I'll do what I can to interest Father in the visit. What time should we arrive?"

"The Johnson family should arrive before dinner, so Father suggested Friends come anytime after the noon meal.

I can't wait for them to arrive. I get so anxious for news from outside East Grove!" Betty said emphatically. "Oh-they also have a daughter who is fourteen. She is still attending school, so perhaps she can give us some new ideas for our lessons!"

We both left school on Friday with an air of anticipation. The weather was exceptionally warm for the end of April; indeed it felt more like mid-summer.

Perhaps the weather had something to do with Father's good spirits, for he was more than agreeable about visiting the Jessops on Saturday. Mother and I would take pies made from the last of our dried apples. Abigail was the only member of the family who was less than excited about the upcoming visit.

"There will be no one there my age," she had complained when I spoke that night about the Johnsons. "Thee will be with Betty, and the boys have each other to play with, but I will end up sitting with the women! she moaned, as if it were a sentence worse than prison!

"Betty and I will talk with thee, and the Johnsons have a fourteen year old daughter—perhaps she will want to play with thee. There is also the fact that Betty's father invited anyone in meeting to attend, so more than likely there will be Friends there thee knows!" I said encouragingly.

"I doubt it," Abigail said, continuing to feel sorry for herself.

"Then thee can talk to Betty and me! Now—no more self-pity! Thee needs to learn to enjoy thyself when a chance to

117

*FOR THE LOVE OF A FRIEND*

visit others arises!" I scolded gently.

When there was no response, I decided Abigail had either fallen asleep or was unhappy with my admonition. I refused to let her self-pity dampen my good spirits. I couldn't wait until our trip!

I knew it was going to be a great day when the sun's warm rays gently woke me. Remembering our afternoon visit to the Jessops, I hurriedly dressed so as to help Mother with the pie-making. To my surprise, the pies were already baking in the dutch oven hanging over the fire when I came down from the loft!

"Good morning, Rebecca! Thee must have been a bit tired from thy long week at school!" Mother smiled warmly as she checked the baking pies.

"I am sorry I slept so long," I said, shocked, when I realized how late it was.

"I was happy to let thee enjoy thy sleep, Rebecca. Thee has so little chance to catch up from thy short nights during the school week. When does thee think Betty will want to finish school for the year?" Mother asked.

"We were discussing the matter this past week, and Betty will announce after meeting on Sunday that there will be just two more weeks of school. We have already lost several of our older students who have had to help with breaking the sod on their farms. Betty and I both felt a need to continue as long as possible since we did not get started until November."

"I know thy father will be glad to have Jacob home again for sowing the wheat and oats. He would never keep him out of school, though, unless it were an emergency. He knows the importance of schooling." Mother paused, then continued, "And has thee noticed Jacob has not asked once if he could stay home from school to help?!"

"Betty has done a wonderful work in that boy's life," I praised, "Jacob is almost a model student, and he really has a

118

sharp mind! His abilities have surprised even me!"

"And Levi," Mother asked, "how has he progressed under thy teaching?"

"Levi has been a delight!" I said fondly of my little brother. "He loves to read almost as much as Abigail, and is quick with sums. Abigail continues to be one of the top students in every area, of course. She can spell even better than I, though I do not wish for her to know that fact!"

"I have great hopes for my children," Mother began, speaking to no one in particular, "and I know their education is the foundation for those hopes. I feel so blessed to already have thee in the teaching profession, Rebecca, especially when thee can nurture thy own brother! Betty says thee is wonderful with the young children!"

"So thee has been talking to Betty, has thee?!" I said teasingly. "And just what else has she had to say about me?"

"Only that she doesn't understand thy treatment of Joshua Frazier. And frankly, Rebecca, I don't understand it either," Mother finished with a puzzled look.

How do you explain something you sometimes don't understand yourself? My feud with Joshua had begun years before the trip west and had simply continued after our move to Iowa. Not wanting to try and explain to Mother, I simply said, "Joshua has been a help to us at school, and I have tried to abide peacefully with him as much as possible."

I kept pondering Mother's question as the morning progressed and we began our trip to the Jessops. Perhaps it was time I buried the hatchet with Joshua. If the opportunity presented itself, I would try and make peace with him once and for all.

As we approached the Jessop's homestead, I quickly scanned the group of young people gathered outside to catch a glimpse of this Luke Johnson Betty had spoken of. The first person I saw was Joshua, (wasn't he always!) but then I noticed a tall, golden-haired young man speaking with Betty. When he turned, I could see why Betty had been anxious for

*FOR THE LOVE OF A FRIEND*

his visit. Luke Johnson was the most handsome man I had ever seen! His deep blue eyes were nearly as dazzling as his smile! Hurrying from the wagon, I proceeded to the now laughing group.

"How art thou?" I greeted no one in particular.

"Rebecca, I would like for thee to meet Luke Johnson from Pleasant Plain. Luke, this is Rebecca Wilson. She and I teach together at East Grove School," Betty finished the introduction.

"Pleased to meet thee, Rebecca. Betty has told me many things about thee, as has Joshua as well," he said, glancing quickly with a grin at Joshua.

Now what in the world could Joshua have told Luke about me already, I wondered angrily?

"Thee cannot always trust Joshua's words to be truth," I said quickly, hoping for the best.

"Oh, his words were only of the highest form of praise for thy snake—charming abilities!" Luke said with a laugh.

Forgetting my earlier vow to make peace with Joshua, I lashed out, almost before I realized what I was doing.

"Joshua Frazier, when will thee put the past behind thee? Thou art a spiteful boy!" I spat out.

"Why don't we play a game?" Betty asked quickly, seeking to prevent a heated argument between Joshua and me.

"Yes, let's have some fun," Luke joined in. "When I return to Pleasant Plain, I will need to concentrate on my work. But today I would like to enjoy myself!"

"What type of work does thee do?" I couldn't help but ask, my never ending curiosity once again getting the best of me.

"I am apprenticing as a carpenter, Rebecca. There is a need for one who can build the simple furnishings Friends need, as well as wagon wheels and other farming items. I believe it will be a service to those in my community. I will soon be eighteen and have a business of my own," Luke finished proudly.

"Luke is a wonderful craftsman," Betty said warmly,

*New Beginnings*

"Look what he fashioned for me!"

Betty withdrew a small wooden box from her skirt pocket. The lid had been intricately carved with delicate flowers and butterflies. It was truly beautiful.

"That is a wonderful keepsake, Luke. Thee must be very talented!" I said honestly.

"Thank thee, Rebecca. I believe God has given me a love of working with wood few men have, and I feel fortunate to have a life work that I enjoy so much. Of course, there are some negative aspects of my profession."

"What is that?" Joshua asked.

"Coffins. I have great difficulty building a box to lay another human being in, especially when it is someone I have known," Luke finished solemnly.

Not only was this young man good looking, he was also compassionate!

"How about a game of tag?" Luke suggested, eager to return to more pleasant matters.

"Yes, that's a great idea!" I joined in.

"Why Rebecca! I thought thee did not play childish games!" came Joshua's teasing words. That boy had the memory of an elephant!

"I do not mind playing with adults, Joshua," I threw back at him, immediately regretting it. Why did I always have to get in the last word? Perhaps now was as good a time as any to begin my peace-making efforts.

"I'm sorry, Joshua," I said carefully. "That was not a kind remark, and I should not have said it."

For once in his life, Joshua Frazier was speechless. In fact, he seemed almost embarrassed by my apology. Smiling to myself, I quickly joined in the game. Making peace with Joshua had been far more effective than all the sharp words I had ever spoken, I thought with satisfaction.

I was determined to enjoy myself whether Joshua was present or not. Luke Johnson made tag fun, teaching us new ways to play the old familiar game. Glancing toward the

*FOR THE LOVE OF A FRIEND*

cabin, I noticed Abigail talking and laughing with a girl I had not seen before, but who I presumed to be Luke's younger sister. I was happy she had found someone to share the day with, as we would have that much more to talk about on the ride home.

Before we knew it, Betty's father was calling us for a time of refreshment. Several women had brought pastries, a special treat for many of us.

Seeing Betty trying to shoo the persistent flies away from the desserts, I went over to visit with her. "Where is thy mother?" I asked when I realized I had not seen her all afternoon.

"This was not one of her good days, I'm afraid. She has never fully recovered from her illness this past winter, and Father and I are really quite worried about her, though we try not to let it show. There are days when she does not rise from bed, yet other times she seems like her old self. I would really appreciate thy prayers for her, Rebecca," Betty finished, an anxious note in her voice.

"Why hasn't thee mentioned this to me at school?" I asked when I sensed her deep concern.

"I didn't want to burden thee with my trials, Rebecca. Father and I keep praying God will heal her."

"I still wish thee had shared thy concern with me, Betty. I could have been praying for her, as well as for thee. Now that I think about it, she hasn't been at meeting much since the new year began," I added, more to myself than Betty.

"I really am worried, Rebecca. What would our family do if something happened to her? She means so much to each of us!" Betty was near tears as I moved to embrace her.

"But my God shall supply all your need," I quoted, realizing just how difficult it was to fully trust in God's promises, especially when it involved someone you loved. "God will take care of thy mother, Betty. We will just have to trust Him."

"I know thee is right Rebecca, but how would thee feel if

122

*New Beginnings*

it were thy mother?" came her pointed question.

I couldn't answer. Her question put a different perspective on the matter. If it were Mother, I would no doubt feel the same as Betty: worried and completely helpless.

Wiping her eyes, Betty began to pick up the remaining pastries. "Let's pass these around and see if anyone wants another serving. Then we can watch Luke and Joshua pitch horse shoes with the other men."

That sounded good to me. And maybe it would help take Betty's worried mind off her mother. Watching the men throw horse shoes wasn't my idea of great fun, but it would be rewarding to cheer for Luke in the hopes he would win—especially if he were to compete against Joshua! That would be a wonderful finishing touch to an already great day. Maybe Luke would even visit again sometime, and his family would also be at meeting tomorrow.

I was the happiest I had been since arriving in Iowa, our first year now nearly complete.

# Chapter 16

# Gurney versus Wilbur

The meeting house was filled as we began our worship service the next day. It was always a good feeling to have so many Friends joining together for the common purpose of worship. Betty, and Luke Johnson's mother and sister were sitting directly in front of me, so I presumed the rest of the family was on the mens' side. A feeling a sadness crept through my soul when I realized Betty's mother was once again absent from Meeting. Praying for her recovery would be one of my first tasks this morning as we sat in the silence. This was also the day for monthly meeting, so it was with added anticipation that I prepared for what the day might hold.

I was surprised to see Mrs. Johnson rise to speak midway through our time of silent worship, although East Grove Friends always welcomed other Friends to speak when led by the Spirit.

"It is with great concern that I speak this morning," she began. "God has spoken to my heart, and I feel I must share with you the words He has given me. As many of you are aware, we at Pleasant Plain have made plans to begin a time of weekly Bible instruction before our regular Sunday meeting for worship. When my husband and I were living in Indiana, we traveled to Richmond to hear Joseph John Gurney speak, whom many consider to be the most influential Quaker in the British Isles. It was because of this man's inspiration that we came away with an increased awareness of the

125

FOR THE LOVE OF A FRIEND

importance of teaching our children about the Word of God. We have carried this concern with us to Iowa, and will soon see the fruits of our labors when our Sunday classes begin. Joseph helped all of us see the importance of God's Word in our lives, as well as the need for more Bible Study. Many of you also know of the teachings of John Wilbur from the New England Yearly Meeting. He feels Joseph Gurney's emphasis on the Scriptures is misplaced and Friends are losing their peculiarities. I strongly feel John Wilbur is sowing seeds of discord among Friends, and I would urge you to unite with us who recognize the importance of the Holy Scriptures. We are not dismissing the Light of God within the human soul. We are simply reiterating the beliefs of the founders of the Society of Friends: the ultimate source of truth is found within the Word of God and confirmed by the Light within. I would ask you to make this a matter of prayer in your meeting, perhaps beginning a similar time of instruction of your own if you feel so led."

I had a growing respect for Luke's mother as she sat once again. I had heard Father speak of Joseph Gurney many times in the past, and I knew he had great respect for this man's teachings. We would have much to ponder as we worshipped this day.

The men must have had a similar voice in their meeting, for Joseph Gurney and John Wilbur were the main topic of conversation among the young people gathered to share our noon meal. As we bowed for silent grace, Clyde Jessop admonished all Friends present to remember the significance of breaking bread together, the act of communion commemorating the Last Supper of Christ. As Friends, we did not pass a loaf of bread or glass of wine, but felt the breaking of bread at the noon meal was every bit, if not more meaningful.

"I think Joseph Gurney is the greatest Quaker since George Fox!" Joshua began excitedly as we were seated on the blanket Betty had had the foresight to bring.

For once I had no quarrel with Joshua's words, although

126

*Gurney versus Wilbur*

I doubted he had the knowledge some of the older members possessed on the subject!

"I was fortunate my father allowed me to go with him to hear Gurney speak when he was in Richmond," Joshua added, "and I have never heard such a challenging speaker as this Friend! I would think all of us would benefit from more outside speakers—if we could get any to come to Iowa, that is!"

"But Joshua," Mark Mendenhall spoke up, "doesn't thee feel that every believer is a minister of God, able to speak the words of the Holy Spirit to those in need? And if thee believes this, why would we have a need for outside speakers in our meetings?!"

When Joshua didn't answer right away, Luke came to his defense.

"I think Joshua feels as thee, Mark, that all Friends truly are ministers of God. But we also feel there are special gifts the apostle Paul spoke of, one of which is the gift of evangelism. A man such as Joseph Gurney possesses this gift which he uses to exhort Friends to be on fire for God, seeking to spread His Word to all unbelievers."

"But what about this John Wilbur, Luke?" Betty asked. "Does thee feel he is an evangelist as well? It seems to me he is causing discord among Friends when we have long been recognized as people of peace!"

"I feel as thee does, Betty," Luke said, looking at her admiringly. "I fear John Wilbur will cause Friends much pain before he is finally silenced—if that time ever comes. We can do our part, however, if we will follow the leading of Joseph John Gurney. In particular, we can start times of instruction at our Sundays meetings, as well as Bible Studies conducted among families in the areas close enough for easy travel."

"How would these Sunday schools be much different from our primary school?" I couldn't help but ask. "We have a time of Bible reading and prayer every day the children attend, so wouldn't that be sufficient attention to the Scriptures?"

*FOR THE LOVE OF A FRIEND*

"Rebecca is right!" Mark spoke again. "Reading the Scriptures in school should be adequate exposure. The Inner Light of God within each of us was George Fox's message, and I for one feel Gurney is overstepping his bounds by coming to America and using his oratorical powers to influence Friends!"

Mark was really agitated at this point, and Luke spoke again to ease the tension.

"Thee is certainly entitled to thy opinions, Mark. I am certain the last thing Joseph Gurney would want is for us to take sides on this issue! As Betty said, Friends are a peace-loving people, and to disagree to the point we become enemies is certainly not what any of our founders would wish to happen! I would like to invite any of you who wishes to attend our meeting when we begin conducting Sunday School next month. And to answer thy question, Rebecca, it will be different from your time of Scripture in school because we will be seriously studying the Word of God, trying to apply it to our lives rather than merely reading it. Young children need to know about Jonah and the big fish, but they also need to know how their lives may be similar to Jonah's, and how they can avoid making the same mistakes he made!"

Luke was a powerful speaker himself, and when he had finished, nearly everyone spoke of their intention to visit Pleasant Plain Meeting before the summer was over. Even Mark indicated somewhat of an interest in journeying to Luke's meeting sometime.

As Luke's family prepared for their long trip home, everyone gathered around the loaded wagon. It had been such an enjoyable experience having them in our meeting that I felt a lump form in my throat as Luke came over to where Betty and I were standing.

"I want to thank thee for thy kindness to my family, Betty," Luke said sincerely. "I will continue to pray for thy mother's recovery, and for thee as well. Please send word to my family should her condition change."

128

*Gurney versus Wilbur*

Turning to me, he continued. "I enjoyed meeting thee, Rebecca. Betty speaks so highly of thy friendship and how well the two of you have worked together at the school. Even Joshua feels thee is a wonderful teacher!"

This was a surprise, as Joshua usually made fun of my new ideas for the school. Betty had probably been singing my praises to him, which would account for this unusual compliment.

"I hope to see you both in the near future," Luke finished as he turned to leave. "I hope your families will visit Pleasant Plain sometime this summer as well, so I will say 'farewell' for now, but not forever!"

"Farewell!" Betty and I said in unison, both saddened by their departure.

When the dust from the road was the only visible sign of the Johnsons, we turned back to the task at hand: packing all the dinner items in the wagons and preparing for Monthly Meeting.

The matter of starting a time of instruction before Sunday worship was brought up in monthly meeting by both the men and women in the afternoon. No action was taken, however. as there was no consensus on the matter. I was certain it would be brought up in next month's meeting, and also confident it was only a matter of time before East Grove Friends Meeting would begin a Sunday school with the purpose of studying and applying the Scriptures.

"Rebecca, why is thee so quiet?" Abigail asked as we traveled the now familiar road home.

"I suppose I am a little sad that the day is over, as well as the Johnson's visit. Luke Johnson was such a pleasure to be with, and I'm just sorry he's gone home," I said rather forlornly.

Abigail had a surprised look on her face, but perhaps she knew this was not the time to tease me about Luke. I could only hope our family, particularly Father, could be persuaded to make a trip to Pleasant Plain in the not too distant future!

129

*FOR THE LOVE OF A FRIEND*

The topic of Sunday schools was introduced again by Father as we shared in our family time that evening.

"What did thee think of the Johnsons' support for Joseph Gurney's idea of a Sunday time of Bible teaching?" Father asked, looking at Mother.

"If thee is thinking of our children, Alfred, I do not believe it would harm them. The time we spend reading and discussing the Scriptures each evening, however, should make it unnecessary to hold special classes before worship each week. Rebecca, what is thy feeling on the subject? Is it thy opinion the children are adequately taught at home and school?" Mother asked me.

I was torn as to how to answer. I did not want to disagree with Mother, but I felt a strange loyalty to Luke as well. Should I try to stay neutral on the subject for Mother's sake, even though I felt more strongly in favor than against? I finally decided I needed to be as honest as possible and hope Mother would not feel that I was betraying her.

"When Luke Johnson first mentioned the idea of a Sunday school," I began, "I was reluctant to accept it. I felt like thee does, Mother, that there is enough instruction given in the family and school to make it unnecessary. But when I listened to Luke speak on the subject as we were breaking bread together, I began to see his point of view. He feels we read the Scriptures, but don't directly apply them to our lives. He believes children need to learn how to apply stories like Jonah and the big fish to their own lives so they won't make the same mistakes he did!" I finished, quoting Luke nearly word for word.

"I suppose there might be some truth to what thee is saying," Mother replied, "but I certainly hope Abigail, Jacob, Levi and thee have had adequate teaching on the Scriptures here at home!"

"Oh we have!" I quickly added, not wanting to seem ungrateful for their patient instruction. "Father and thee have done a wonderful job as parents! But not every family spends

*Gurney versus Wilbur*

the amount of time we do with the Scriptures. And I suppose that was the deciding factor in my support of a Sunday school. There will always be children in our meeting who do not have the benefit of the kind of home we have had, and it would be for those children we would conduct the Scripture lessons each Sunday."

"I believe thee has a valid point, Rebecca," Father finally answered. "I did not speak in meeting today, but I believe I can speak with a clear conscious on the matter next month. I may also try to visit those who were not supporting the idea before next monthly meeting to try and gain their support."

This was the first time I felt Father had truly sought my opinion on a subject, and it felt good. As I would soon turn sixteen, I suppose in his own way Father was encouraging me to think and form opinions for myself. Mother looked pleased as well, and it was a good feeling to know I had not disappointed her with my words.

Abigail and I had another one of our late night conversations as we discussed our fun-filled day.

"I am glad thee encouraged me to go to the Jessops on Saturday," she began. "I really like Lydia Johnson, and she invited me to visit her at Pleasant Plain. Does thee think Father will let us visit this summer?"

"I hope so! I really like Luke, too, and it would be a fun journey to their home."

"Does thee like Luke?" Abigail asked. "I mean, does thee really like him?"

Not wanting to discuss my feelings toward Luke just yet, I was reluctant to answer. Finally I said, "I like Luke a lot. He is very intelligent, as well as good-looking. We are just friends, though."

When there was no reply, I decided Abigail had fallen asleep. With Abigail now wanting to see Lydia again, there would be another person to help persuade Father to visit the Johnsons. The prospect would give me something to look forward to as the summer progressed.

**Chapter 17**

# Signs of Strength

With the dismissal of school for the summer, my days seemed to drag by. Each morning as I awoke there was an emptiness within me, and it was difficult to stay home and perform chores for Mother. I had never dreamed I would miss my students so, and I was already looking forward to the beginning of the next schoolyear. But it was Betty I missed most of all. We had become so close as the school year progressed, and it was as if a part of me was missing each day. I had no one to share my innermost thoughts with, no one to encourage me or laugh with me. As much as I hated to admit it, I even missed Joshua! His constant attention to the physical needs of our school had meant seeing him nearly every day, and we seemed to progress to the point of peaceful cohabitation.

The middle of May marked the end our first year in Iowa. It was hard to believe so much had happened in the span of twelve short months. If I had tried to envision my first year in East Grove, I could never have dreamed of the emotions I would come to experience. There had been John Shipling and my decision to remain with Friends; becoming a teacher instead of a student; surviving a blizzard while saving Matthew's life, and the fellowship with the wonderful Friends at East Grove Friends Meeting, Betty Jessop in particular. If Father had given me the choice of staying in Richmond or

133

*FOR THE LOVE OF A FRIEND*

moving to Iowa, I doubt I would have made the journey west. Now I was so thankful he had not given me that choice, for I would have missed out on the blessings of my new life.

Father and Jacob had intended to break another twenty acres of sod this spring to expand our planting acres. The sod was extemely difficult to work, even with the steel breaking plow. Roots extended deeply into the soil, tangling with each other in a solid maze. Each evening Father returned exhausted from his labors. The oxen were likewise weary from their struggle to pull the plow through the tough earth. Even Jacob, whose job was mostly keeping Father company, climbed to the loft early each night for much needed rest.

Though the work was extremely difficult, I never heard Father complain. I often wondered if he ever regretted leaving his job as overseer of a large warehouse in Richmond. I knew he felt it had been God's call which brought him to Iowa, but I couldn't help but wonder if he wished he were back in Richmond. To toil with the plow as Father did each day required mental as well as physical strength. There was also the matter of the weather—never knowing if a hail storm, drought, or early frost would wipe out the year's labors. It took a great amount of faith, I decided, to enjoy the life of a farmer! All these thoughts were wandering through my mind as Mother, Abigail, Levi, and I worked in the garden, sowing seeds I had not even known existed! Mother and Father had made a special trip to Salem to purchase garden supplies, and Mother had made the most of it! As I finished the last row of beans, I heard Jacob shouting at the top of his lungs.

"Mother! Rebecca! Mother! Rebecca!"

Realizing something terrible must have happened, Mother quickly dropped her seeds and took off running as fast as her heavy skirts would allow. I did likewise, knowing Jacob would not be yelling unless it were an extremely important matter!

Jacob's face was pale with fear as we reached him, and his labored breathing made it difficult to understand his words.

134

The two words we did understand, however, were 'Father' and 'hurt'. No wanting to waste any time, we all began running toward the field where Father and Jacob had been plowing. In the distance we could see the form of Father lying on the ground, lifeless and still. My heart was in my throat as Mother and I finally reached his twisted body.

"Alfred! What is it?!" Mother sobbed, kneeling over her husband.

"Oh...my leg! Oh...my leg!" Father moaned over and over again.

Looking closely, we could see Father's leg in the furrow the plow had cut, in what looked like a deep hole. The leg was twisted grotesquely, indicating a serious break.

"What do you want us to do?" Mother ask imploringly.

"Thee...will...have...to...pull...the...leg...out...of...the...hole," Father managed, agony evident in each word.

"Rebecca, I don't think I can do this alone!" Mother pleaded. "Please help me!"

Sensing Mother needed additional strength, I realized it would be best if I took charge of the rescue.

"Thee will need to steady Father while I pull his leg from the hole," I began. "Then we will make a drag for Samson on which to pull him back to the cabin. Jacob, I need thee to get two of the rails from the fence around the cow shed and the sheet from Mother and Father's bed. Tell Abigail to bring Samson to the field as well."

Jacob quickly ran toward the cow shed. From the expression on his face, I knew he was grateful for the chance to help in some way, anything that would help take his mind off the terrible sight of Father's pain.

I began the unpleasant task of removing Father's leg from the deep hole. Being as careful as possible, I began to try and pull out the twisted limb. Because of the way Father had landed, the leg was immovable, held in the hole by the pressure from the weight of his body.

"We will have to move Father before I can free his leg," I

*FOR THE LOVE OF A FRIEND*

told Mother. Positioning ourselves on either side of him, we found the strength to slide the torso into a position more in line with the leg. Father was nearly unconscious by now, the pain having taken its toll. Gently lifting the leg, I struggled to release it from the hole's grasp. Without Father's assistance, the dead weight of bone and muscle was almost more than I could manage. Praying for strength, I continued to carefully maneuver the limb until it was finally free. Father continued to moan in pain, while Mother moved her lips against his white cheek, no doubt asking God to ease the pain of this partner she so dearly loved.

Jacob helped me fashion a make-shift drag with the poles and sheet. Fastening them to Samson's harness, we began the slow and agonizing journey to the cabin. Abigail and Levi were crying, silent tears of fear, for they had never seen their Father in a position of weakness. Mother walked along side the drag, holding Father's hand in an effort to comfort him. Every bump we passed caused more moaning, and I knew something would have to be done once we reached the cabin. But what? Should I send Jacob for the doctor in Salem? It was a long ride, and there was no assurance the doctor would be there when Jacob arrived. I knew the leg was fractured, but I did not think it had broken the skin. If that were the case, we could probably fashion a splint for the leg which would allow it to heal properly. I hoped Father would not lose consciousness so I could ask him what he wished me to do!

We finally had Father in bed, though getting him into the cabin had not been easy. It had taken all five of us working together to carry him on the sheet. Somehow knowing I had taken charge of the situation, Father began to speak to me.

"Rebecca...thee needs... to set the bone... in my leg. Thee needs to...pull...on my... foot until...the bones line up," Father gasped with a great deal of effort.

Knowing I had to do as he asked, I went to the foot of the bed. "Mother, thee and Jacob will have to hold Father's body so there will be pressure on the bone. I will count to three and

136

*Signs of Strength*

then pull."

It took three tries before we heard the bone snap into place. Father had lost consciousness, the pain being more than he could bear. I instructed Jacob to cut one of the split rails into two pieces to fashion a splint. Using scraps of material from Mother's sewing, we tied the rails on either side of the leg.

"Will he be all right?" Mother asked anxiously.

"I think he will be fine in time," I said gently. "He will be in a great deal of pain for several days, but if he stays off the leg, it should heal nicely." Keeping Father off the leg would be no easy task, but we would deal with that problem when the bone began to heal.

"Jacob, thee needs to go to the field and bring the oxen in. Can thee do that?" I asked.

"Sure, Rebecca. I will do the rest of the chores as well. But how will we get the field plowed?" he asked, voicing the question haunting my own mind.

"We will find a way, Jacob. We will find a way! God will supply our needs," I answered with more confidence than I felt.

How would we plow the field? Father would probably tell us to work the ground he had already broken and leave the rest for another year. But I knew we needed the extra acres for our family's living expenses, so I would just have to find a way.

"Maybe we could ask Joshua Frazier to help us," Mother began.

"NO!" I said fiercely. "We will NOT ask Joshua for any help! It will get done," I promised, "It will get done!"

The question of the field continued to burn in my mind as I tried to sleep that night. Father had regained consciousness and had even eaten some soup Mother prepared for him. Though still in excruciating pain, I knew he would do all he could to hide that pain from his family. An idea had wormed its way into my mind, but I had no way of knowing if it were possible. Could I plow the field? The fact that I was a woman would not stop me. Women could do anything men could do

137

*FOR THE LOVE OF A FRIEND*

if—and this was a big if—they were physically strong enough. I was not as large as Father by any means, but my shoulders were broad and I was more heavily muscled than many girls my age. I did not think Father would approve if I were to present the idea to him, but there would be little he could do or say if the acres were already plowed when he discovered my plan!

I dreamed of plows and furrows that night, and when morning came, I knew I had to try and plow the field. When breakfast and chores were finished, I called the others outside the cabin, away from Father's listening ears. I explained my determination to plow the field, and to my surprise no one doubted the possibility!

"Jacob, thee will need to bring the oxen to the field and show me how to handle the plow. The rest of you will need to take Father's mind off the plowing and off me. You will need to make excuses for my absences while I am in the field."

"Is thee sure thee can manage the plow?" Mother finally asked, knowing the work needed to be done, but not willing to risk injury to another member of the family.

"I will do my best, Mother. I believe God will give me the strength necessary to guide the plow. Jacob will assist me if I cannot manage alone."

As we headed for the field, the expanse needing to be plowed seemed to have doubled in size since the day before! How had I ever thought I could plow such a large field?!

When Jacob had the oxen hitched and the explanations given, I was ready to begin my farming career, however short it might be. At first the plow wanted to come out of the ground in spite of my determination to keep it deep in the sod. The oxen were a great help, knowing exactly where to walk to keep the plow in the dead furrow. I knew we were moving at a slower pace than I had seen Father plow, but this was as fast as I would be able to go. If it took a month to plow the field, it would just have to take a month!

After the first hour or so, it seemed to get a bit easier. I had learned how to keep the plow down in the sod, though my arms ached constantly. Teaching school did little to prepare one for hard physical labor!

Each night I dropped into bed, some evenings too tired to even eat supper. But the area of field to be plowed continued to shrink every day as my confidence grew. It felt good to accomplish a goal, even if the pace was extremely slow.

On the day the last furrow was plowed, I sank to my knees in the rich black soil and thanked God for giving me the strength to accomplish the impossible! I had plowed nearly an entire field, and I was proud of my labor.

I was certain Father knew of my efforts after a few days, but he had said nothing to discourage me. He had been moving around the cabin with the help of a pair of crude crutches Jacob had fashioned from two saplings. The leg appeared to be healing, and the pain that remained was no longer severe.

As Jacob and I were cleaning the plow the day after we finished the field, a single horse and rider appeared on the horizon.

"I wondered how long it would be before someone grew suspicious about our absences from meeting," I told Jacob.

As the figure drew nearer, I could see it was Joshua. Much to my surprise, it was almost a pleasure to see him.

"How art thou?" he inquired, climbing down from his horse.

"I am fine, thank thee. How art thou?" I said in reply. "We have been wondering why thy family has not been in meeting the last few weeks."

"Father has broken his leg," Jacob answered, not supplying any details.

"I am sorry to hear of thy misfortune," Joshua said sincerely. Then looking out over the newly plowed field he added, "It is lucky he finished breaking the sod before his accident!"

"The field was not even half done when he stepped in the hole!" Jacob retorted, much to my chagrin.

*FOR THE LOVE OF A FRIEND*

"Then..how.." Joshua seemed to be at a loss for words. "Then how did the field get plowed? Did Friends come to thy aid? I did not hear anyone mention the field at meeting!"

"Rebecca did it!" Jacob burst out proudly.

I will never forget the look of unbelief which crossed Joshua's face. Realizing Jacob would not make up such a tale, he finally broke into a grin.

"Rebecca, thee is the most remarkable girl I have ever known! Guiding the plow would have been a formidable task for a man thy age, let alone a woman!"

I knew Joshua was trying to pay me a compliment, so I decided not to take offense at his disregard for the abilities of women!

"It was not easy," I said honestly, "but it had to be done and there was no one else to do it."

"Would thee object if the other men of the meeting would gather to harrow and plant the seed?"

This was a change in character for Joshua. He usually acted first and asked later!

"I believe Father would appreciate the crop being planted. I know it is nearly too late to plant now, so if a good crop is to be raised we will surely need some extra help."

"I will spread the word to those in the area and we will plan a day in the near future to get the seed in the ground."

"I would appreciate that, and I'm sure Father would as well. Thank thee for wanting to help us."

"I would do anything for thee, Rebecca. Doesn't thee know that by now?!

I turned away as I felt the heat creep into my face. Why did Joshua have to say things like that? He knew our past differences.

"Would thee mind if I spoke with thy Father?"

"What...about?" I stammered.

"About where to plant the crops," he said gently.

Now I was throughly embarrassed. "Go on in the cabin," I said stiffly, turning to walk quickly back to the plow.

140

*Signs of Strength*

A thorn in the flesh. Joshua was my thorn in the flesh that the Apostle Paul had written of. Perhaps I needed to speak with him about Betty Jessop. If he had someone else to associate with, perhaps he would leave me alone.

Somehow that prospect did not bring the happiness I expected. What was I going to do with the likes of Joshua Frazier?!

**Chapter 18**

# Love is Blind

Father's leg continued to heal nicely as the summer progressed. He was careful to keep his weight off the mending bones in hope they would be healed enough for the fall harvest. When Friends in the meeting had heard of his accident, they made sure someone was present when work on the crops needed to be done. Once the fields were planted, they returned in July to harvest the oats and wheat, and would help with the corn in October, if necessary.

We children were kept busy helping Mother with the garden; in fact, it seemed there was a new crop to harvest every day! We had dried many times the number of fruits and vegetables prepared the previous summer. Although the stringing of the produce was a tedious job, it would be well worth our efforts come fall.

I still had not forgotten the invitation to visit Pleasant Plain issued by Luke Johnson back in April. In early summer when Father's leg was still mending, I did not think it wise to suggest a long journey. But when August arrived, I decided the time had come to bring up the subject.

"Father," I began as we finished our evening meal one night, "does thee remember the Johnsons' visit to East Grove last April?"

"Well, I do recall something of the visit! It was my leg I injured, Rebecca, not my mind!" he said with a smile.

143

*FOR THE LOVE OF A FRIEND*

"What I meant was, does thee remember the Johnsons' invitation to visit their meeting and see their new Sunday school?"

"Yes, Rebecca, I have been thinking of making the journey for several weeks, but I did not know if my leg could stand the rigors of several hours on the road. It is still painful if I happen to bump it or accidently put my weight on it."

This was the first time Father had mentioned his pain since the accident. I knew he had suffered greatly after his fall, but I admired his courage as well as his determination to keep the pain from the rest of his family.

"I'm sorry thee had to suffer, Father. I suppose we will have to visit Pleasant Plain some other time," I said, trying to keep the disappointment from my voice. By some other time, I knew I was really saying next summer as it would be too dangerous to travel during the winter, and fall and spring would be busy months in the fields.

"Does that mean thee would not want to travel the last of this month if my leg feels up to it?" Father asked slyly.

"Of course I would like to go!" I said eagerly.

Soon the others were entering the conversation, the prospect of a trip, even to Pleasant Plain, was enough to excite us all!

"I would rather you didn't get your hopes up," Father cautioned us all, "as my leg might be reinjured, or rainy weather might set in, or any number of circumstances could arise to keep us from traveling. But if everything works out, we will plan to make the trip the last Saturday and Sunday in August. Rebecca, thee might want to ride Samson to the Jessops and see if they would take word of our possible arrival when they go to Pleasant Plain next week."

"I didn't know the Jessops were going to Pleasant Plain next week!" I said, surprised that Betty had not mentioned it to me at meeting the Sunday before. Now that I thought about it, whenever I had mentioned the Johnsons to her, she had acted rather strangely and changed the subject! Why would

144

*Love is Blind*

she want to keep her visit a secret?

There was only one way to find out. "I'll ride over to visit Betty first thing tomorrow. I have been meaning to pay a call on her mother anyway." With the exception of one Sunday, Betty's mother had been unable to attend meeting during the summer. The day she did attend, she looked so weak it nearly broke my heart.

I tried not to become too excited about our possible trip to Pleasant Plain, but it was impossible not to think about it. It would be so good to visit with Luke again, and I was anxious to see how they conducted their Sunday Bible instruction. It would also be fun to meet some other Friends my age.

Hurrying through my chores the next morning, I was soon on my way to Betty's cabin. It was a beautiful morning, but I knew the brightly burning sun was a prelude to a hot afternoon. When I reached the cabin, Betty was nowhere to be seen. The homestead looked a bit run down, and I knew Betty must be having trouble doing all the work her mother would normally have done. A feeling of guilt overcame me as I wished I had thought to offer Betty my help. After all she had done for me, it would have been the least I could have done.

"Betty!" I called. "Where art thou?"

"Out here in the garden!" came the familiar voice.

Walking to the garden, I saw Betty pulling the onions. She would tie them together and hang them to dry before they had a chance to rot in the ground. We had done the very same thing a few days earlier.

"It is so good to see thee!" Betty exclaimed, throwing her arms around me in a tight embrace.

"I have missed thee so much since school was dismissed!" I confessed to her. "How is thy mother?"

The smile vanished from Betty's face, replaced with a look of sorrow. "Not well, I am afraid. Father finally summoned the doctor from Salem, but he said there was no medicine to cure her problem. He thought she must have contracted a respiratory disease last winter that permanently

145

FOR THE LOVE OF A FRIEND

damaged her lungs. It is terribly difficult for the lungs to get the oxygen her body needs, which causes her great weakness." Betty sighed, as if resigned to the illness.

"I'm so sorry, Betty!" I said sincerely. Then I remembered Father's words about the Jessops possible trip to Pleasant Plain. "But what about traveling to Pleasant Plain? Will thee and thy father go alone? Who will take care of thy mother?"

"Mother insists she can travel the few hours it will take to get to the Johnsons. She wants to go so badly that I think Father is going to take her, as sort of a last wish," Betty finished with a sad note.

It hurt me to realize that for all practical purposes, Betty had resigned herself to her mother's passing on, although I knew there wasn't much else she could do. Our prayers for her recovery were not being answered; at least not in the way we wished. One of the hardest verses in scripture for me to accept was Romans 8:28: "For we know that all things work together for good to them that love God, to them who are the called according to his purpose." How could the death of a loved one work for good, especially such a wonderful Christian witness as Mrs. Jessop.

Whatever Betty's reasons, I decided not to inquire as to why she had not told me of their upcoming trip. She had probably been worried about her mother and simply forgotten to mention their plans.

"I almost forgot the reason I came!" I exclaimed. "Our family is planning to visit Pleasant Plain also, on the last weekend in August. Father was wondering if thee would ask the Johnsons if this would be suitable for them. We would arrive after dinner on Saturday and stay for the Sabbath. Abigail can't wait to visit Lydia again, and I am looking forward to seeing Luke."

I noticed a strange look cross Betty's face before her slow answer.

"I would be happy to inquire about thy visit when we travel to Luke's. He speaks highly of thee, and was amazed when he

146

*Love is Blind*

heard thee had plowed twenty acres after thy father's accident!"

How had Luke known about Father breaking his leg and my plowing? I did not know news traveled that fast here in the territory! And when had Betty seen Luke again?

"When did thee see Luke?" I couldn't help but ask.

Blushing slightly, Betty said, "He stopped on his way to Salem a few weeks ago. He was anxious to know how Mother was feeling, and he wanted to thank our family for the wonderful time they had in April. He also wanted to make sure we planned to visit them so they could repay our hospitality." I thought maybe there was more she wanted to say, but decided not to make an issue of it.

"Is thy mother able to visit for a bit?" I asked, knowing I shouldn't stay too long.

"I'm sure she would be pleased to see thee," Betty replied as we began to head toward the cabin. "She misses meeting so much and it always means a great deal to her when Friends are able to visit."

I was not prepared for the shrunken form of the woman lying in bed. In no way did this body resemble the strong woman I had first met at our cabin raising. Her once healthy body was now merely a skeleton, and I did not know what to say.

"Rebecca!" came the warm words always spoken from this saintly woman. "How nice to see thee again!" She smiled and paused, her breathing labored. "How is thy family?"

I told her all about Father's accident and how the rest of us had tried to carry on the work.

"I understand completely," she said sadly. "It has been such a burden on Betty and her sister to try and do my work. I would do anything if I could only get out of this bed and go to the garden!"

"Now mother," Betty spoke softly, "Thee knows we can take care of the garden. It is not a hard job at all!"

When there was no reply, we quietly rose to go back out.

147

*FOR THE LOVE OF A FRIEND*

Betty's mother had drifted off to sleep and we did not want to disturb her with our chatter.

"If thee will give our message to the Johnsons, I will check back with thee after thy return," I said when we had caught up with the news and I was preparing to mount Samson for the trip home. "Have a good trip! Maybe it will be good for thy mother to see other Friends."

"Thank thee, Rebecca. And thank thee for coming this morning. I wish we could visit more often, but I know we both have extra responsibilities with our families right now. I am looking forward to the new school year when we will see each other on a regular basis!"

"And I as well!" I said fervently. "Farewell, Betty."

"Farewell, Rebecca."

I couldn't get the picture of Betty's feeble mother out of my mind on the ride home. I had a dark feeling she would not be with us much longer unless a miracle were to occur. I believed in miracles, but I wasn't sure I had the faith to believe it would happen to Betty's mother. I spurred Samson on, willing the wind rushing past my face to dry the rapidly falling tears. Why did this have to happen to such a wonderful woman as Mrs. Jessop? Why? Why? Why?

The Jessops were able to make the trip to Pleasant Plain, much to my surprise. Mrs. Jessop even seemed a bit better after the trip. Betty had spoken to the Johnsons about our visit, and they had been more than anxious for us to come. Father felt his nearly mended leg could stand the journey, so we began to anxiously prepare the food and belongings we would need to take for overnight. As this was the first time in over a year we would be gone from home for more than a day, it was cause for great excitement.

Though I saw Father grimace a few times, he seemed to survive the trip rather well. We had no trouble locating the Johnson homestead as Luke had given Betty a map to help us

148

*Love is Blind*

find our way. Lydia and Luke came running to meet our wagon, nearly a quarter of a mile from the cabin!

"Greetings!" Luke began. "Did you encounter any problems on your journey? How is thy leg, Alfred?"

"We had quite a good trip, actually," Father answered. "My leg was not a problem—except when the horses steered the wagon through areas of deep ruts!"

"Mother and Father are waiting for you at the cabin," Luke continued. "We might as well take the wagon there and get your belongings unloaded."

Lydia had climbed in the wagon beside Abigail and they were chatting amiably, trying to catch up on the past four months. I couldn't help but stare at Luke. He was every bit as handsome as I remembered, those blue eyes sparkling as he spoke. I would have to get to know this man better, I vowed!

The Johnsons had built an addition to their cabin specifically for guests. It seems they were in the habit of inviting Friends for visits, and had wanted them to be as comfortable as possible. Mr. Johnson made the comment that they had had someone visit every weekend but one throughout the summer. I admired their wonderful hospitality. That would be the sort of thing I would like to do when I had a home of my own.

Luke was polite throughout the week-end, but any efforts I made to get to know him better seemed futile. He must have something on his mind, I finally decided. Something he did not want to share with me.

I was greatly interested in their Sunday school during our Sabbath visit to their meeting. The members had been divided into age groups with one adult teaching each class. Even the adults had a class and teacher. The children seemed to enjoy their activities, and if they learned as much as I had in my class, it was certainly an idea whose time had come! Luke was our teacher, and his knowledge of the Bible was amazing.

"I thought you were a carpenter, not a theologian!" I said half teasingly as we were on our way home.

Luke smiled. "Just because one is a carpenter by trade does

*FOR THE LOVE OF A FRIEND*

not mean he must be ignorant where the Word of God is concerned! I have spent a great deal of time studying the writings of George Fox, Robert Barclay, and Joseph John Gurney, to mention a few. Their interpretation of scriptures seems to apply so well to our lives today! Has thee ever read any of their writings?"

"No, I guess I haven't," I said, thoroughly embarrassed. Here I was the school teacher, yet my knowledge of Quaker philosophy was limited to what I had heard at meeting.

"I could loan thee a few volumes of their works, if thee is interested."

"I would like that very much," I said, vowing to know more the next time I saw Luke Johnson. And there would be a next time! There had to be! This was a man I admired a great deal, just the type of man God might be sending my way!

As we said our farewells, Father invited the Johnsons to pay us a visit in return. Mr. Johnson promised to try and come back to East Grove sometime within the next year, as he had promised to visit the Jessops again as well.

"Farewell, Luke!" I added, smiling warmly. "Will we see thee again soon?"

For just a moment, Luke seemed to be at a loss for words. Finally he said, "I'm sure we will be in contact again soon, Rebecca. Have a good trip home!"

Luke's parting words seemed to echo in my mind throughout the long journey back. What had he meant by 'being in contact'? Would he come alone for a visit soon? Maybe it meant he would come calling in our home!! I would have to keep that thought to myself as I didn't want to be misinterpreting his words!

Father and Mother chatted warmly about their visit, both marveling at the success of the Sunday school. Abigail and Jacob were discussing Lydia, and I thought I noticed a new interest in the girl on Jacob's part. Surely he was not interested in her as a girl! He was nearly twelve, so I supposed it was not impossible. Levi had fallen asleep, as usual. I almost missed

150

*Love is Blind*

his "when will we be there" questions! This left me alone with my thoughts, which continued to include a certain tall, blond-haired young man. But I would be careful with love this time, and not make the same mistakes I made with John Shipling.

Sixteen promised to be an exciting age! Perhaps I was maturing into a woman after all! I hoped so, and I hoped Luke thought so as well!

# Chapter 19

# Till Death Do Us Part

As the days grew shorter and cooler, one could really sense the approaching fall. Once again Abigail and I worked with the potatoes, nearly doubling our crop of a year earlier. I smiled as I watched Levi haul the crates of potatoes to the cache pit behind the cabin. My thoughts went back to last year's potato harvest when I had sent Levi after Jezebel. Jezebel was still with us, and we continued to graze her in the south woods. Levi had grown and matured so much in the past year that it was now his job to take the cow to new pastures each day. He had explored the south woods so many times he knew it like the back of his hand and never got lost again. He was growing by leaps and bounds, looking more like Father every day. Though he would still be under my tutelage this year at school, it would be the last. Betty would surely enjoy him when he became her student.

Father's leg continued to improve, allowing him to walk with a cane. He was confident he could harvest the corn crop with our help after school and on Saturdays. Father had thanked me personally for taking charge of his rescue the day he went down, and for acting so quickly and efficiently. I knew he was also thankful for the plowing I had done, though it was harder for him to accept the fact that I, a woman, had done a man's work. Perhaps he felt guilty for having broken his leg thus halting the field work. It was enough for me to know he was grateful to have the work done.

*FOR THE LOVE OF A FRIEND*

I had ridden Samson to Betty's home nearly every week since the first of September, as we had much planning to do for the upcoming school year. Betty did not wish to leave her mother alone so we agreed to meet at her cabin.

There were days when Mrs. Jessop seemed improved; she would chat with us about school and meeting. On other days, however, she was silent, appearing to be asleep. I knew Betty was grieving for her mother. She had trouble remembering what we had just discussed, always keeping one ear tuned to the sound of her mother's breathing. Had I thought it would help, I would have made the preparations for school myself. It was Clyde Jessop who assured me that coming to the cabin to make plans for school was the appropriate thing to do.

"I am so glad thee has been coming to work with Betty," he had told me one day when I rode up to the cabin. "She has become so involved in her mother's illness that I sometimes fear for her own well being! Thee is just what she needs to help her remember she has responsibilities other than caring for her mother!"

I tried my best to involve Betty as much as possible with the school plans. I knew when October arrived and we began teaching the students, Betty would be glad we had taken the time to prepare beforehand.


Having seen the frail condition of Mrs. Jessop the last few times I traveled to the cabin, it was not a surprise when Joshua came riding to our home the last day of September with the news that Mrs. Jessop had gone to be with the Lord. Knowing Betty would need my help the next few painful days, I prepared my belongings for a stay at the Jessops until after the funeral. I had never been closely associated with death before. No one in my family had died since I was a young child, so I did not exactly know what to expect. I just knew I had to go.

Explaining my plans to Mother, I quickly loaded my few belongings and rode to the Jessop cabin. Once I arrived, however, I wasn't sure what was appropriate. Should I quietly enter the cabin without knocking? What if they were praying, or mourning as a family? The decision was made for me when Clyde appeared at the cabin door. Seeing my bag, he nodded and motioned me to come in. "It is well thee has come, Rebecca. Betty needs thee now more than ever."

Walking into the cabin, I felt a sense of peace instead of the darkness and sorrow I had expected. Betty quickly rose from beside the still body of her mother and I took her in my arms. When we parted, I was surprised to see a smile on Betty's face.

"Thank thee for coming, Rebecca. I knew thee would be here for me and my family! Mother is with the Lord now, and her suffering is over. It was the suffering which grieved me so these last few months. Thee knows I would have done anything in my power to keep her alive, but the pain she endured was more than I could bear at times. I feel so fortunate she had the Light of Christ within her soul and now walks with Him on high!"

I had come expecting to comfort Betty, but it was Betty who was the comforter. What a remarkable young woman she was! When I thought of Maude, my best friend back in Richmond, and some of the silly conversations we had regarding boys and such, I realized what a difference there was in a mature relationship with someone such as Betty!

Although Betty insisted I return home, I persuaded her to let me stay to help with the meals and funeral preparations.

"Has thy father made all the arrangements for Tuesday?" I asked. This was the day set for the funeral.

"I believe he has," Betty said, quickly looking away. "The coffin should arrive sometime tomorrow morning, and Friends will call tomorrow afternoon. Then Tuesday we will take the coffin to the meeting house for the service."

Imagine my surprise when the wagon bearing the coffin arrived on Monday. The driver was none other than Luke Johnson! Betty walked slowly toward the wagon, the plain board coffin indicating the finality of the occasion.

*FOR THE LOVE OF A FRIEND*

Luke took Betty in his arms, a look of tenderness in his eyes. "I am so sorry! I know how much thee cared for thy mother!"

"Thank thee, Luke. I will always be grateful for the work of thy hands to build her coffin. I wasn't sure thee would receive word of her death in time, but Friends assured us the message would be delivered, so we proceeded with our plans."

There was a look in Betty's eyes I had not seen before. Perhaps it was only gratitude. Luke had taken the time to build a special coffin for her mother, traveling through the night to deliver it in time.

Luke finally noticed me standing in the doorway and nodded.

"Greetings! How art thou, Rebecca? It is good to see thee again," he called, walking with Betty to where I stood.

"It is so good to see thee!" I said warmly. Then realizing the solemnity of the occassion, I added, "I am just sorry it is not for a happier reason!"

"Actually," Luke began, "I do believe this is a happy occassion! When someone such as Betty's mother leaves her earthly body to be clothed in a heavenly one, it can only be a time for rejoicing! I believe Betty feels as I do."

Smiling appreciatively at Luke, Betty agreed. "It is a happy occassion for the believer, though my life will never be the same without Mother." Tears were shining in her eyes, but she didn't seem sorrowful.

Clyde helped Luke unload the coffin and place his wife's body in the box. He was bearing his grief well, but I sensed the pain within as he prepared to say farewell one last time to the woman he dearly loved.

Friends arrived that afternoon to express their sympathy to the Jessops. I tried to stay in the background, talking with Betty's sister, or simply watching the various Friends minister to the Jessops. Luke also sat away from the family, though I noticed his eyes seemed mainly to be focused on Betty.

*Till Death Do Us Part*

The funeral on Tuesday was conducted in the manner of Friends. The coffin had been borne from the Jessop home to the meeting house in silence. Friends believed funerals were occasions for deepest reflection on the life of the deceased, as well as their own lives. As family and friends sat in the silence, those wishing to speak of the life of the departed Friend could do so, as well as those who wished to pray. In due time the coffin was carried to an open grave in the cemetery next to the meeting house where another period of silence followed. Friends were expected to reflect on the uncertainty and shortness of life and the need to prepare for death. No gravestone would be placed on the grave, just a simple marker that would tell the world this Friend was no longer in the body, but with the Lord in heaven.

Silence followed as Friends slowly left the grave sight. Betty rode back to her cabin with her family as I did with mine. The Johnsons had made the trip from Pleasant Plain, and they would return to the cabin, as well as several other families close to the Jessops.

Betty and I had prepared a bit of refreshment for Friends facing a long journey home, and serving the others helped keep my mind off the image of the coffin in the open grave. It was not until I saw Mother standing with Father that the finality of my dear friend's loss become reality. Sobs began to wrack my body as I quickly walked to the far side of the cabin. I hoped no one had seen my sudden departure, for I had no desire to talk yet.

Just as I turned the corner of the cabin, my heart sank as I saw Betty and Luke in an embrace that was considerably more than comforting! Hoping they hadn't heard me, I quickly moved back around the corner. Luke's voice, though low, carried easily to where I stood. I knew I should leave, but somehow my feet refused to move.

"Betty, I have loved thee since the day we first met!" Luke exclaimed. "I know God led our wagon to thy cabin when we could not find the way to Salem!" When there was no response

157

*FOR THE LOVE OF A FRIEND*

from Betty, he continued. "I know this is not the proper time, but I am so afraid I will not see thee again for many weeks to come. I don't know how to approach the subject except to say I would consider it a great honor if thee would consent to be my wife!"

Carefully looking once again at the couple, I saw the tears in Betty's eyes were tears of joy, not sorrow, as she simply nodded her head. "I have loved thee for some time as well," she finally said, "and I would consider it a great privilege to become thy wife. Thee knows we will have to have the approval of our parents and both meetings, but I believe we are both well thought of by the Friends of each meeting."

"Perhaps we should keep our news to ourselves until a more appropriate time," Luke said reluctantly. "Just know I would like nothing better than to tell the world thee is going to be my wife! I just wish thy mother could have known of our plans!"

With a shy smile on her face, Betty replied, "I think she had a good idea! Until the day she met you, she had been trying to interest me in Joshua Frazier. I always had a fondness for Joshua, but it can not compare to the feelings I have for thee! Mother and I had a number of conversations as she lay on her sick bed, and you were often the topic of our discussions!"

A grin broke out on Luke's face as he fervently kissed his wife to be. Realizing others would be wondering where we all were, I made my way to the front of the cabin. My tears had dried, but the ache in my heart cried out. Betty's actions the past few months were easily explained by the scene I had just witnessed. Perhaps if I had not been so blind, I would have known Betty and Luke were falling in love. As I rounded the front corner of the cabin, I nearly ran over Joshua.

"I have been looking for thee for the past ten minutes!" he said anxiously. "Is thee all right?"

The floodgates burst open once again, and I did not protest when Joshua took me in his arms. "It will be all right, Rebecca," he soothed over and over again.

158

*Till Death Do Us Part*

Just then Luke and Betty emerged, hand in hand, and Joshua knew the source of my tears. "I'm sorry, Rebecca. I know thee had an interest in Luke, and I guess I should have told thee about him and Betty."

Pushing him away, anger overtook the original pain.

"Thee knew Luke and Betty were interested in each other and thee did not tell me?! I thought thee was my friend!"

"I'm sorry," he said again. "But I didn't think thee would believe me if I told thee! I presumed thee would just think I was trying to trick thee into liking me!"

Joshua spoke the truth. I never would have believed him.

"I'm sorry, Joshua. So many things have happened today, and I just can't deal with them all."

Walking quickly to the cabin, I got my belongings and headed for Samson. I had no desire to see Luke and Betty so happy, and I could not bear to have Joshua see my pain. Signaling to Father that I was leaving, I headed down the road to home.

What was going to happen next? Twice I had allowed myself to develop feelings for a man, and twice I had suffered because of those feelings. And what about our school? If Betty were going to marry Luke, would she still be the head teacher? There was no way I could handle twenty children on my own!

I knew there would be questions about my sudden departure when the others arrived home, so I quickly made my way to the loft and into my bed. At last free to let go of my feelings, the hot tears once again flowed as the darkness settled over the cabin and my soul.

## Chapter 20

# Peace and Promise

With only one week before school was scheduled to begin, I knew my strained relationship with Betty would have to change. The more I had thought about her involvement with Luke, the angrier I had become. I had thought we were best friends. More than that, even. I thought we were as close as two women could be, able to share our innermost thoughts and feelings. But I had been wrong. Betty had been falling in love with Luke for months with nary a word to me. That was what hurt the most. I felt the warmth rise in my cheeks as I remembered the times I had confided in her of my interest in Luke. She must have had a good laugh at my childish behavior, knowing Luke was already falling in love with her!

I still couldn't believe I had been so blind where Luke was concerned. There were so many times he was hesitant, almost stuttering over his words when I would mention Betty. When he had said he would be in contact following our visit to Pleasant Plain, I had actually thought he might be going to ask Father's permission to call in our home! How could I have been such a fool?

Seeing Betty at meeting the Sunday following her mother's funeral had been like rubbing salt in a wound. I made sure I sat in the back for worship and headed for the wagon as soon as the service was finished. When I had glanced toward the meeting house, I had seen Betty look my way with a very long

161

*FOR THE LOVE OF A FRIEND*

face. She made no attempt to come to the wagon, however; maybe she was beginning to realize how much I had been hurt by her lack of trust in me. As far as I was concerned, she could marry Luke and move to Pleasant Plain and live happily ever after!

I knew I was bitter and hard to live with. I was trying to finalize preparations for school, though I didn't even know if Betty would be teaching. The meeting would just have to hire another teacher if she had other plans. Mother and Father seemed to understand my unhappiness, though Abigail, Jacob, and Levi were not so patient.

"Thee is an old grouch!" Jacob remarked one evening. "I hope the old Rebecca returns before school begins!

Levi quickly came to my defense. "She is not a grouch!" She just isn't very happy. She is a good teacher, and she likes her students!"

Throwing my arms around Levi, I hugged him tightly for his loyalty. Looking at each of my siblings, I knew I owed them an apology. It was not their fault I was so hard to live with!

"I'm sorry I have been so unpleasant these past few days. I guess I am just feeling sorry for myself. Will you all forgive me?" I asked.

"What is the problem?" Abigail asked curiously.

"Rebecca's life is her own to deal with," Father said firmly. "We will not interfere unless she wishes."

"I think I'll retire early, and maybe tomorrow will be a better day!" I finished lamely.

Abigail continued her questioning when she came to the loft a bit later, but I was in no mood to discuss my friendship with Betty—or in this case lack of—with Abigail or anyone else. When I didn't answer, Abigail must have assumed I was asleep because the questions stopped. I had thought so much about my situation the past few nights that my brain refused to

162

*Peace and Promise*

consider one more "might have been." Slipping into sleep, I dreamed of weddings and funerals; neither of which were mine.

With school to begin in two days, I began to feel anger replacing my other emotions as I sat at the table trying to finalize my teaching plans. Betty was the head teacher. Why hadn't she let me know what we were going to do? After all, she was the one who had kept the secret; she was the one responsible for my hurt; and she was the one about to marry and move away. At least she could have paid me a visit with news of her plans!

"Rebecca, Betty is coming!" Jacob interrupted my thoughts, yelling from outside where he was helping Father build an addition to the cow shed.

So she was finally doing what she should have done a week ago! I had surely been wrong about Betty Jessop!

Riding slowly to the cabin, Betty dismounted and walked to the door of the cabin. "May I please speak with Rebecca?" I could hear her ask when Abigail answered her knock. "Come in, Betty," I said stiffly

Walking straight to where I sat, Betty knelt beside my chair. I could see the tears in her eyes as she took my hands in hers.

"I'm sorry, Rebecca. Can thee find it in thy heart to forgive me?"

"There is nothing to forgive thee for!" I answered bitterly.

"Even if there weren't, thy unhappiness is reason enough to seek forgiveness!"

Feeling the walls of my defense begin to crumble, I asked the question that had haunted me since the day of the funeral.

"Why, Betty? Why didn't thee tell me about Luke? I thought we were friends! I thought we could share every-thing! I told thee of my trials with John Shipling!"

"Yes," Betty said slowly, "but as I recall it was several months after the problem."

"But thee knew I was interested in Luke! Thee let me carry

163

*FOR THE LOVE OF A FRIEND*

on and on about our visit to Pleasant Plain and how handsome I thought he was, while all the time thee had already captured his heart! A good friend would not have let me believe in something that could never happen!" I said in anguish.

"I am truly sorry! I wanted to tell thee about Luke, but I wasn't sure of his feelings toward me. I was afraid if I told thee I was interested in Luke, it would drive a wedge between us. I was correct, wasn't I?" she asked gently.

Knowing there might be some truth to her words, I finally realized what an awkward position I had put her in. But why hadn't she come to me immediately after my discovery of her and Luke and explained her behavior to me? I could have been more forgiving if I hadn't had to suffer the past week wondering what the future held.

Betty soon answered my question. "I wanted to talk with thee at meeting that Sunday after Mother's funeral, but when thee left for the wagon immediately after the service, I was afraid thy anger would be great and I did not want to argue on the Sabbath. The next day, Luke came back and took me to his home to spend some time with his family. We also wanted to inform both the men and women's meetings at Pleasant Plain of our intentions to marry. Each body is required to appoint a committee of two to investigate the suitability of our marriage. Luke knew this process was going to take some time and he was anxious to get it started."

"Will thee have to do the same thing at East Grove?" I asked, becoming more interested in the details.

"Yes, we will appear before each of our meetings here as well. If everyone approves, we will publicly declare our continued intention of marriage and suggest a wedding date. Each meeting will then appoint two members to oversee the wedding." She paused, then added, "I hope they choose thee as one of the members! If thee would consent, that is!"

"I would be happy to help thee, Betty. I'm sorry my behavior has not been very Christ-like since I accidently overheard Luke declare his love for thee. It hurt so much, and

164

I thought thee did not consider me a friend worthy of thy confidence! I suppose thy reasons make sense, though I hope I would have had the grace to accept thy feelings for Luke."

"I truly am sorry I did not confide in thee, Rebecca. And I do hope thee will forgive me."

"I do. And will thee forgive me as well?"

Rising from her kneeling position, Betty hugged me tightly to answer my question.

"But what are thy plans?" I finally remembered to ask. "What about the school? Will thee move to Pleasant Plain? Will I have to teach alone?"

Smiling broadly, Betty's next words were exactly what I needed to hear. "That's one of the things I came to tell thee! While I was at Pleasant Plain, Luke and I spent many hours discussing our future. Since he has just begun to build his carpentry business, he feels it would be best for both of us if he were to move to East Grove after we marry and begin a new business here. Since Father still needs my help, we will live in the cabin with him and my sister. Isn't that wonderful? We can still teach together and best of all, we can still be good friends!"

"That is wonderful!" I said honestly, truly happy for her and Luke.

Why hadn't I waited to talk to Betty before jumping to some of the wrong conclusions? I suppose this would be another lesson I would learn from my friendship with her. I just wished I were more like this loving woman.

"When does thee anticipate the wedding will be held?" I asked, my excitement beginning to build.

"Luke believes we will pass meeting before the year is out, and he will propose a date as soon after that as possible! The wedding will be so exciting, but the best part will be sharing my life with Luke! My only regret is that Mother will not be here to witness our happiness."

We continued to talk of the wedding, nearly forgetting the most important matter at hand: school! How fortunate we had

*FOR THE LOVE OF A FRIEND*

spent those earlier days at Betty's cabin making plans. Once again the excitement of starting a new school year began to bubble within me as we took care of last minute details.

Peace reigned in my soul that night for the first time in months. All of life was indeed a sacrament if one were open to experiencing God's grace!


December first dawned crisp and cold, though the bright sun gave the illusion of warmth. Today was Luke and Betty's wedding, and I was truly happy for them. Each time I saw them together I realized the depth of their love for each other. I could only hope for the same some day in my own life.

I had been thrilled when the meeting selected me as one of the two overseers for the wedding. Normally the older members were chosen for this honor, and I had a feeling Betty did a bit of talking to the selection committee to secure my position! Helping Betty with the plans had been difficult, however, as the emptiness in my own life seemed to grow with each passing day.

There was a stillness in the air as we approached the meeting house for the wedding. When everyone had gathered, we entered in silence with Betty and Luke moving to the front. A time of worship followed with several members rising to speak highly of one or the other of the two young people about to take their vows. In due time the Clerk of Meeting, Clyde Jessop, gave the signal for Luke and Betty to say their vows.

> Rising and taking Betty's hands, Luke spoke first, "In the presence of the Lord, and before this assembly I take thee, Elizabeth Jessop, to be my wife; promising with divine assistance to be unto her a loving and faithful husband, until death shall separate us."

Betty then repeated her vows to Luke. A marriage

166

*Peace and Promise*

certificate was produced with all present signing as witnesses of the sacred act. After checking for accurateness, Clyde Jessop returned the certificate to the newly wed couple.

We continued to remain silent, following Luke and Betty to the Jessop cabin for a special wedding dinner.

What a difference a few months made! Once again I was helping Betty serve the guests, but this time there was a truly joyous atmosphere. Just seeing the way Luke looked admiringly at Betty from time to time was enough to tell the world this was a marriage ordained and blessed by God.

I had long since lost my feelings of anger and jealousy. I was happy for my good friend, and so grateful she would still be living in East Grove.

As I made one last trip for water to wash the dirty dishes, I was intercepted halfway back up the path by Joshua.

"Would thee have a drink of water for a thirsty soul Rebecca?" he asked kindly, a twinkle in his eye reminding me of the day of the cabin raising when I offered a drink to him and John.

Joshua had changed a great deal in the past eighteen months. Not only had he finished growing physically, but a good deal of the teasing had disappeared as well. Now that I thought about it, I had not heard the name "Becky" for a good many months!

Joshua had been such a help at school, and I knew he was well thought of in the meeting. Could the man God was preparing for me have been right by my side all these months and I had been too stubborn to even realize it? Or was I imagining things again?! Joshua probably had no interest in me whatsoever after the way I had treated him since moving to Iowa.

"I would love a drink of water!" Joshua's spoke again, his words interrupting my thoughts.

Pondering that possibility, I took the dipper from the pail and began to collect the water. Taking the bucket from my hand and setting it on the ground, Joshua gently enfolded me

*FOR THE LOVE OF A FRIEND*

in his arms. When he felt me return the embrace, his next words revealed his true feelings. "Does thee know how long I have wanted to hold thee like this?"

"Thee has a strange way of showing thy fondness, Joshua!" I couldn't help but say.

"I know I teased thee a great deal. But I didn't know how else to get thee to notice me! First there was John Shipling, and then Luke Johnson! What else was I to do?!"

So even Joshua had noticed my interest in Luke. Did everyone in East Grove feel sorry for poor Rebecca Wilson and her lost love?

Blushing fiercely, I looked at Joshua. There was no look of pity in his eyes, only admiration. When I didn't reply he finally asked the question it had taken him six months to get up the courage to ask: "Does thee think thee might like to have me call on thee in thy home—if thy Father has no objections, of course?"

Did I want Joshua Frazier, at one time the most despised boy I knew, to come calling

Looking at the man he had become, I knew the answer. Perhaps I would indeed enjoy the company of Joshua Frazier. "Yes, I would like that," I said simply, words I never thought I could ever say

I had come to Iowa with many conflicting emotions, all of which had eventually been overcome. I had spent a great deal of time and effort trying to know God's will for my life, seeking to find the love of a Friend. I had a feeling I was about to experience that special kind of love. A warmth slowly began to fill the emptiness in my soul as Joshua took my hand and we began the walk back to the cabin.

168